# • SHEILA MILLER •

## I Can Trace a

# Rainbow

Overseas Missionary
Fellowship
1058 Avenue Road
Toronto, Ontario M5N 2C6

## AN OMF BOOK

5.25

*Books by the same author:*
The Shark's Fin Five
Tara
My Book About Hudson
I went to school... in the jungle
Pigtails Petticoats and the Old School Tie
Ian and the Gigantic Leafy Obstacle
TZ 3

© OVERSEAS MISSIONARY FELLOWSHIP
*(formerly China Inland Mission)*
Published by Overseas Missionary Fellowship (IHQ) Ltd.,
2 Cluny Road, Singapore 1025,
Republic of Singapore

*First published .... 1987*

*OMF BOOKS are distributed by*
*OMF, 404 South Church Street,*
 *Robesonia, Pa. 19551, USA;*
*OMF, Belmont, The Vine,*
 *Sevenoaks, Kent, TN13 3TZ, UK;*
*OMF, P.O. Box 177, Kew East,*
 *Victoria 3102, Australia;*
*and other OMF offices.*

ISBN 9971-972-60-3

Printed in Singapore                    10.AU87KHL

# CONTENTS

*for*
*John*
*who, hand in hand,*
*has traced the rainbow's arc with*
*me.*

# *Foreword*

Some of the greatest missionary books ever published came from the China Inland Mission. No society has been so blessed with faith-building writers. Indeed, it has been said that as many lives were influenced by those books as by the missionaries. Today, the Overseas Missionary Fellowship continues the high literary tradition with many titles, its best-known writer in recent years being Isobel Kuhn. "Is Sheila Miller possibly her successor?" we asked as we read these pages. Certainly, not since reading Isobel Kuhn have we been so inspired by an OMF publication.

Yet to describe I CAN TRACE A RAINBOW as a missionary book would be inadequate. Here is a glimpse of the poignancy of all human life. This is the story of a talented young couple's response to God, about the bright and grey days, the intensity of a mother's love and its sacrifice, of disappointments and unexpected provisions. We laughed and smiled and cried and suffered with the writer, sharing her enjoyment of Siamese cats and wool and home and shopping and beautiful things.

It made us want to pray more intelligently, to give more spontaneously, to listen more alertly each day for God's whisper. In these pages there is beauty, pain, faith, shattered hopes, blue skies and a Heavenly Father who tenderly cares for a small uprooted family.

I CAN TRACE A RAINBOW put a song in our hearts and gave us a new understanding of God's special people—the missionaries.

*Ann and Edward England*

*O Joy, that seekest me through pain,*
*I cannot close my heart to Thee;*
*I trace the rainbow through the rain,*
*And feel the promise is not vain*
*That morn shall tearless be.*

George Matheson

# 1

## Blue turns to grey

The doctor's tall figure stood framed in the surgery doorway. His appearance was grim. Battling with a desperate sense of anticlimax, I heard him say to my husband, "Mr Miller, there is no point in giving you a medical examination for your wife will never be accepted by any missionary society."

We stumbled out of the waiting room into the September sunshine — but the bright bubble of expectancy had burst. The train journey back to London was dead — dead as the frozen ambition to be missionaries.

The Essex countryside, bathed in the golden glow of approaching autumn, glided by. How radiantly the Creator had painted the landscape; yet how drab was the atmosphere trapped in that grey carriage. The panorama from the windows was flat yet glorious because of the coming of fall. Myself, I preferred a prospect with depth — hills and hummocks and braes, like the craggy slopes in the Scottish Cairngorms or the gentle Connemara ridges of our native Ireland, the icy Alpine peaks or, yes — the jungly mountains of

Malaysia! Malaysia. That vision had been so vivid — a school in a little green valley, tucked away in the peninsula's highlands. It needed teachers. God was calling. We were qualified to go.

"Well, perhaps we're not meant to," John ventured. His voice cut into the heavy discouraged silence as the train rattled towards London.

"But that was our final interview," I said. "Everything had gone so well in the other six."

"We can't join a missionary society without thorough medicals — so that seems to be it." A pause hung between us before John added, "Did he not examine you at all?"

"No. Just looked at my papers and then in a slow, measured tone, he said, 'Mrs Miller, do — you — seriously — think — any — missionary — society — would — touch — you?'"

My voice sounded choked.

"What did you say?"

"I told him I knew I had been ill but I considered that to be all in the past. He obviously wasn't impressed."

Silence fell again in the sunny compartment. It was difficult to come to terms with the thought that the dreams had evaporated. That lovely valley. All those missionaries' children. We had thought the whole idea such an adventure — an adventure with God.

Ideas. Perhaps my bother in life was that I had too many. Knock down a sitting-room wall? Run a home Bible study group? Take a writing course? Be a Tupperware demonstrator? I kept wondering what to do about the question marks.

To teach had been my first ambition. For years I had been imparting knowledge — first to imaginary children and then to real boys and girls, including our own little seven-year-old son. I thought that this first-ever idea had been all in God's plan to prepare me for teaching in the school in the jungle. Up until today it seemed to me that the pieces of life's jigsaw had been fitting neatly together in recent months.

The possibility that I might be wrong was rocking me.

Inwardly I began to retrace what had been our pointers towards missionary work — right back to the evening when Mr Mooney had visited our home in Ireland. I had been regaling him with an idea I had about starting a church library. I was keen to know God's will about it. I'll never forget the advice he gave. "If the idea is not from God," he said, "it will fade away and come to nothing. But, if it's from Him, the thought will gain momentum and the idea will grow."

So praying about question marks became a principle of mine. When an idea hit me, I would begin to talk to God about it. Often ideas hadn't been mine at all; the Lord had put the thought into my head.

Idea number one thousand and one was: couldn't we be missionaries? Now this impression, though most recent of the lot, was neither really new nor sudden. I'd always wanted to be a missionary but somewhere along the line the thought had been lost.

In fact, one of the very first pieces of information I'd ever heard about John Miller was that he, at the age of 21, was thinking towards missions. That little insight, at the time, had attracted me more than ever to this tall, fair-haired young man.

But John and I had managed somehow to bury that idea under a mortgage, wall-to-wall carpeting, a sparkling new fridge, the latest electric cooker (to the chagrin of my father who was the manager of the

Londonderry Gaslight Company), a big beautiful washing machine and our very first brand-new car. And, of course, there'd been the nursery to decorate; Jonathan Neil's arrival to await, the nicest baby carriage on the market to buy.... No wonder the thought of being missionaries became weary waiting for attention.

Then Cecil hit Ireland again.

Cecil had grown up with us in Londonderry. Cecil was the culprit who instigated our first date. He had been groomsman at our wedding. Now he was a member of the Overseas Missionary Fellowship. Four years ago he had set out for Malaysia. Suddenly he was home on leave and all over our house once more, leaving newspapers spread out on every cushion and pins from his new shirts in the dressing table drawers.

*Heatherlea,* our small "semidetached suburban," was cosy with its new central heating. The three of us sat round the fire and talked and talked ... On one of those evenings Cecil fished a prayer letter out of a pocket. "I've finished with this," he said, "You might want to have a look at it."

Seventeen years later he told me that the action had been planned. We didn't know that, though. What if we had? If we'd realized then that this was it? That we were rubbing an Aladdin's lamp leading to adventure with God? Would my fingers have trembled as I reached out for that green page — *The North Malayan Newsflash?* Supposing we'd known that this letter would change the course of our comfortable lives?

Innocent of a destiny crisis, I glanced at the Newsflash. And, right at the end, the typewriter had announced, *"Teachers are needed for Chefoo School in the Cameron Highlands. When missionaries take their furloughs we are short-staffed."*

Chefoo was the Overseas Missionary Fellowship's school for the children of its missionaries. It hung in a green valley, high in Malaysia's mountains.

What a launching pad for ideas! I was ready to set off on the next plane! But I had found that special line of attack about my ideas — we had to talk to God about it first. Eventually, we began tentatively to push the door ajar to give us a glimpse of adventure with God in the Far East. We submitted applications to be missionary teachers at Chefoo School.

Now the train drew into London. Had we been mistaken in our guidance? Had it all been a human impulse? An idea, not from God? We each battled with our chaotic thoughts.

That September morning God seemed to be saying, "No".

Was life like a cassette-recorder on which we'd pushed the fast forward button too soon? Was five years' distance from my illness not long enough?

Life's playback mechanism clicked. I found myself rewinding with it. The tape spinning in my mind reversed swiftly from 1969 to 1964. Dejectedly, in the sunless station, *I* back-tracked too ...

# D i e d  1 9?

If I could know that I must die next year
how well should I prepare for the event!
I'd make a will, pay visits far and near,
take care how every busy day was spent.

Some things I'd burn, and with the rest be free;
I'd pay all debts, keep small amounts in hand,
be reconciled with all my family,
and nearly finish most of what I'd planned.

I'd find my Bible; turn its dusty page;
those half-remembered prayers reclaim as mine,
and once a month, at least, make pilgrimage
towards the old church door — when it was fine.

But since I am not under that dark threat
I do not mean to start all this just yet.

*Christopher Idle*

# 2

# *Shadows*

Jonathan Neil had not been quite two years old when I discovered a second baby was on the way. It was 1964 and I was 29. J-boy was such a bouncy bundle of sunshine that John and I were highly delighted at the prospect of a brother or sister for him. Entirely forgotten were my first gasping words after 22 hours of labour, "How on earth did Mary and Joseph manage in a stable?" It also eluded me that I had greeted John and his bouquet of roses with, "Never again!"

"Early next May," I guessed, counting carefully. "Can you imagine it, John? A spring baby this time. I'll be able to wheel out J-boy's elegant pram again!" The hedgerows would be scattered with cowslips and pale yellow primroses, vetches and ladies' smock; there'd be buttercup fields, bluebell woods ... I'd teach J-boy the names of the wild flowers ... My thoughts rambling happily on, it never occurred to me that anything could go wrong. I mean, that sort of thing always happened to somebody else. Jonathan's birth had been perfectly normal. Instead my mind was full of the pleasure of living on the outskirts of the city where walks into County Londonderry, in the shadow of the blue Sperrin Mountains, were right on our doorstep.

Also right on our doorstep was Europe's most modern hospital — or so people said in 1964.

Time had advanced very little when I discovered in September that I was threatening to miscarry. Immediately John rang the doctor's surgery. "What should she do?" he asked with all the urgency of youth finding life's path suddenly pushing up boulders.

"Depends how much you want to keep the baby," the doctor replied. "If you're keen, better tell her to go to bed and rest."

It was a nonchalant answer but I obeyed. I did want this new baby very much. *Heatherlea's* front bedroom was pink. For a whole month I lay there until I never wanted to see the pretty drapes again.

Towards the end of October our doctor, whom we'd always loved and trusted, decided I'd been there long enough. I was taken across the road to Altnagelvin Hospital.

"Three months, did you say?" queried the specialist. "That must be a mistake. She's big already."

I didn't like that bit. Two years previously I had fallen for any flattery that suggested I was quite small and neat.

Mr Liggett, the surgeon, came to examine me often. "Is there a history of twins in your family?" he asked one day.

There wasn't. But was I excited! A new twin pram. Would they be both girls? Joanne and Judith! I expended the remaining dregs of my energy imagining it all.

Thinking aloud some days later, Mr Liggett

mused, "Perhaps triplets. A multiple birth of some type. I wish I knew what was in there." November's bleak skies clouded the Sperrins then and I was too ill to wonder how one went walking along country lanes with three or four babies plus a two-year-old.

To compensate for loss, I was given a blood transfusion. It seemed to me, in my drugged condition, that the new blood was cold. Icy cold, I thought, as I watched each slow drop flow towards the needle in my arm. Shivering, I asked for a blanket.

Just when somebody noticed that the new blood wasn't right I'm not sure. But the needle was whipped out hastily as I went into a severe shivering attack.

"How odd. Wasn't she Group B+?" asked a doctor. This meant exhaustive blood tests and the search for a donor whose blood would mix with the strange antibodies that had cropped up in mine. Attacks continued. My veins collapsed. It was a nightmare having them probe around with their needles trying to find an inlet for the "washed cells" from yet another new donor's blood.

"You've got the lot," Mr Liggett said one day as I stared at him with yellow eyes. "Oedema now." He raised my swollen feet. When my kidneys seemed to stop functioning, he drew my family aside. "If she doesn't respond by the morning, we'll have to rush her to a machine in Belfast," he explained. "But really, there's nothing more I can do." He said it matter-of-factly but with great kindness. "I must be frank with you," he added. "She is dangerously ill."

"Is there any hope?"

"Very little."

Relatives came and stood round the bed. They chatted to each other. The happy early hospital days, when I picked their brains on crossword clues, were over. My mother sat close, her head on a level with my pillow. I remember her saying, "I would do anything for you, Sheila."

Although heavily sedated, I think I knew death was near. I remember arranging with John about how he should care for J-boy. I remember thinking of Psalm 23 but I couldn't find the Guide to help me through the "Valley of the Shadow".

And then it happened. Afterwards they called it "a torrential haemorrhage". And God, in His compassion, had arranged that a senior nurse was sitting right by my bedside in the morning, at the exact moment it started.

She wound up the end of the bed and whizzed me, like a whirlwind, to the delivery room, dispersing splashes of various donors' blood en route.

"The end of the backache," I thought vaguely. "No more retching and black ejections. This is it, at last."

But there were no triplets; no twins; not even one baby. I passed a thing called a *hydatidiform mole*. That was the day at the end of November, 1964, when my life nearly slipped away.

I'll always think that Altnagelvin Hospital, Londonderry, Northern Ireland is the best hospital in the whole world and that Mr Liggett is the No. 1 specialist.

"Any time of the day or night that you need me," he said, as he arranged me in a new private ward, "you're to call." John and my mother took turns to sit with me at night. In the dim glow of the bedside lamp I would lie watching them struggling to keep their eyes open.

Soon Mr Liggett was examining my inside with his gentle capable rubber-gloved hand. "I'm afraid there's still something there," he said. "A lump. We'll need to operate. Perhaps by Christmas we'll have you ready for surgery."

In all, I had eleven blood transfusions. One day when the drip was out I sat on the edge of the bed and examined my knees. Knobbly. *Funny*, I thought, *I've always wanted thin legs, but now that I've got them, they're ghastly.* I resolved never to disparage my sturdy limbs again — if ever I got them back.

I didn't realize in that month preceding Christmas that if I'd haemorrhaged again it could have been heaven, but I was getting well enough to hear incredible stories from Londonderry's outside world. These little cameos opened up a whole new vista of God's care for me. I knew, of course, of the love of God. Never had there been a time when I didn't know, and I loved Him in return. But now His compassion for His creation became intensely personal.

"Miss Kincaid rang this morning," my mother told me. "Last night she awoke with a tremendous urge to pray for you."

I knew that people were praying but this was different. My loving heavenly Father had awakened one of His servants specially in the night!

"As she was kneeling there in the darkness," my mother continued, "it seemed to her that she shouldn't get back into bed until God answered her prayers. Miss Kincaid told me that she prayed for you until God gave her the assurance that you were going to get better."

"Mr Donaghy telephoned today," said my mother a few days later.

"He said, 'Mrs Rankin, is there anything wrong with Sheila?'

"'Of course', I replied, 'She's been critically ill for three months now.'

"'I hadn't heard about that,' he said. 'However, last night in bed I woke with a deep urge to pray for her. I didn't know why. Mrs Rankin, I feel God is saying she's going to be all right.'

"So you see," my mother concluded, after mentioning the children in John's school and a variety of other folk, "God is prompting people all over Londonderry to pray for you."

I lay there silently, wondering why.

Mr Donaghy came to see me after that. He swung round the 'No Visitors' sign on my door, saying he was my brother. Brother-in-Christ, he meant! "Sheila, God is saying He still has work for you to do for Him on earth," he explained. "He's going to make you well and He'll still be able to use you."

Was there anything I could do for God, I wondered. I felt dreadfully inadequate and besides I wasn't really "spiritual" enough, was I?

Surgery date was December 23rd. That was good-bye to my Christmas dinner! My appetite had been returning and I was putting on weight. The scales now crashed down at 6 stones plus.

Calling John aside before he operated, Mr Liggett said, "I don't know what I might find. Things could go either way ... I just wanted to tell you ..." I realize now that my own lack of concern was due to the prayer that cushioned me and lifted me to soft clouds of oblivion.

The surgeon discovered three tumours — each the size of a baby's head. One on the uterus and one on each ovary. The uterus itself had not regained its shape. Deftly Mr Liggett removed tumours, uterus, ovaries, fallopian tubes and appendix. Years later, in Singapore, Professor Tow was having a look at me.

"That's a superb wound you've got," he said. "Who did that job?"

"A surgeon called Mr Liggett in Ireland."

"Not old Sam? Why, I knew him well in Belfast. He certainly did great things for you!"

He did. But through a haze of pain I realized that Jonathan would never have a baby sister.

"Did you say you already have a child?" Mr Liggett checked some days later.

"Yes," I nodded. "A little boy. He's two."

"Incredible with the state your inside was in. By the way, you'll always need to wear a bracelet to indicate your very rare blood group. Just in case you're ever involved in an accident, you know."

But my thoughts were far away. Supposing I'd never even had J-boy...

*Oh God, thank you.* I breathed. *Thank you for giving me one beautiful big boy before all this happened.*

Shortly afterwards the pathologist's report came from the laboratory in Belfast.

"The outcome of any mole can be predicted in terms of probability of the three classes:

probably benign
possibly malignant and
probably malignant.

I would tend to assign this to the middle group and certainly not to the first ..."

It was January, 1965 when I saw Heatherlea again. I was weak, slender enough to fulfil any aspirations of becoming a model, on the verge of a severe surgical menopause at the age of thirty and of frequent check-ups at hospital for years to come.

No wonder OMF's doctor, five years later, looked grim and stood in his surgery doorway refusing to examine me.

# Rainbows

*I always leave some room*
*for hope —*
*I've known the sky to change*
*from fair, to dull,*
*then back again,*
*all in a single day.*

*I've seen a rainbow*
*span the sky*
*which had been dull,*
*and grey,*
*I always leave some room*
*for rainbows,*
*every rainy day.*

*Karen Rene*

# 3

# A Silver Lining

John's medical problem was his left ear. A burst eardrum, after a childhood attack of scarlet fever, had impaired his hearing. From time to time the ear discharged, so John, in his early thirties, was hospitalized twice for mastoidectomy.

Again we realized that our small semidetached suburban house was pitched on just the perfect plot for the Miller Trio — right opposite that huge modern hospital! Even Jonathan Neil, at the advanced age of two weeks, had tried out its facilities when a virus threatened to affect his eyesight.

It was during his second time as a patient there that John's thoughts were so full of applying to the Overseas Missionary Fellowship. Lying in his hospital bed, he was coming to terms with the fact that a restlessness had crept into his phlegmatic outlook on teaching in Londonderry Model School.

Now as the sun slanted through the hospital's walls of glass, John wondered if after fourteen years of teaching in the same school, his comfortable groove was becoming a rut. And a rut dug deep enough becomes a grave. Supposing we found ourselves middle-aged and nothing to show for it — nothing divinely worthwhile, that is?

The Lord Jesus said that real treasure was storing things up for heaven, not collecting them on earth, but that idea did not dominate our thinking. We hadn't seen beyond the new car, the carpets or the plans for the latest feature for *Heatherlea* — a wall-length natural stone fireplace. Yes, supposing J-boy was suddenly a teenager, what would there be in our lives to prove to God that we loved Him?

Jonathan's Scottish godparents lived in London-derry in the nineteen sixties. Mr Roworth was an architect but the design of his lifestyle lingers more in our minds than the beautiful buildings he planned. One day Mrs Roworth suggested, "This restlessness, John, it could be from God. It often happens that way in a Christian's life."

And shortly after that John found that challenging verse in the Bible which goes:

> "... like an eagle that stirs up its nest
> and hovers over its young,
> that spreads its wings to catch them
> and carries them on its pinions.
> The Lord alone led him ....."
> (Deut. 32: 11-12)

Was the Divine Eagle stirring *our* nest?

*Of course, an ear like mine,* thought John, as he tried to make his bandaged head comfortable on the hospital pillow, could *preclude missionary service.* He knew you weren't meant to live in the tropics if you had a discharging ear. The ear still had a squishy feel about it. Was it going to stay better this time?

A nurse strode briskly into the ward, bright with

its view of the Sperrins. "Time for your dressing, Mr Miller."

Still feeling weak after his operation, John followed her to the surgeon's den. And there, as the ear was swabbed, a remarkable conversation took place between the blue-dressing-gowned patient and the white-coated man with the mirror strapped to his forehead.

John:     I wonder if you could just give me your opinion on whether it would do my ear any harm to work abroad.

Surgeon:   Where do you want to go?

John:     Malaysia.

Surgeon:   It would very much depend on the location of your work there.

John:     Actually I'd like to teach in a school in the mountains — the Cameron Highlands.

Surgeon:   That's where I lived when I was a doctor in the British army. Lovely climate. No problem. It would be quite safe for your ear.

"Think of it, Sheila," John exclaimed when he was safely home in *Heatherlea* again. "Think of it! Of all the ENT specialists who could have operated on my ear, God sent along one who had lived in Malaysia! It's almost incredible!"

So, it was with a real sense of destiny that we had eventually posted our applications to the Overseas Missionary Fellowship. We had checked up on the soundness of John's ear but it never occured to us that my existence (or possible past extinguishment of it) needed explanation.

That's why we were so shattered that day in Essex when OMF's doctor wouldn't look at us.

"I still think five years of good health shows that my illness is over and gone," I complained as we alighted from the train in London. "Why would the doctor not examine me?" Fenchurch Street Station looked drab, and walking out into the September sunshine did nothing to help the grey outlook that blanketed us both like a nimbus cloud.

Even OMF looked dreary that day — the big building at Newington Green where Hudson Taylor had made an arched gateway saying, "HAVE FAITH IN GOD". What was faith anyway? I was always having problems differentiating between my ideas and God's. Now I was deciding that this impression of being led to teach missionaries' children was one of my fantasies.

Yet John had been much more down to earth about it all. He could work out his guidance step by step and he wasn't given to fanciful notions like I was. Was he mistaken too?

The council members gathered that afternoon in an ominous semi-circle to have a final look at us. Our gloom within seemed to shroud them too. We could have passed on the decision for them; they'd shake hands and say, "It's been nice to meet you, but ..."

The fog of uncertainty penetrated that Newington Green office to such a degree that I barely remember what was said. I know they continued the Fellowship's thorough processing and screening of its candidates, but I was far too miserable with disappointment to store most of their queries in my mind.

"Mrs Miller, what do you think of the Charismatic Movement?" one sombre-suited senior citizen leaned forward to ask.

I'd never heard of the Charismatic Movement. I

just felt a failure in every way. Because of me, John couldn't be a missionary. Why were they asking more questions? Had the doctor not told them the worst? My thoughts flew from the greyness of the office to that green jungly valley 8,000 miles away. All those missionaries' children. Chefoo School was still beckoning.

But what was this? The dark-suited quorum was standing. Was it over? Yet they hadn't said, "It's been nice knowing you, but ..." In fact, before we left for home, Dr A J Broomhall, OMF's Candidate Secretary, handed John this letter — a letter we read and re-read and wondered if it could be true.

22 September 1969

Dear John and Sheila

We are grateful to you for the opportunity you have given us to meet you and share with you in seeking the mind of the Lord regarding your service for Him at Chefoo School in the Cameron Highlands.

The committee was unanimous in recommending that you should be welcomed as Associate Members of the OMF in the event of medical approval being received...

With our warmest good wishes and fellowship.

Sincerely yours in Christ
A J Broomhall

I was so impressed about the Lord's handling of things that I decided I'd keep the letter forever — I suppose to prove that I wasn't dreaming! We left London in a daze; bemused, excited. Autumn and Britain were beautiful again. Hope! There was still hope. We were to forward the medical report from my surgeon ...

It is a very naughty thing to ever peek at a doctor's report. Why, I don't know. Of course, my peace of mind might have remained stable had I not looked into that envelope secured from the doctor in Londonderry. To my horror, I saw that Mr Liggett had written,

"It is January 1st, and I am sending Mrs Miller back to you. In this good New Year of ours, may I never see another like her ..."

*Help! This could be the coup de grace,* I thought, but this data was sent to OMF's Medical Officer, Dr Monica Hogben, in Singapore.

It was the end of October before the final news reached us via London:

Dear John and Sheila

I am very happy indeed to be able to tell you that as a result of correspondence between our two doctors — at home and at HQ in Singapore, together with the Assistant General Director, Mr Arnold Lea, the decision has been reached that medical factors need not debar you from serving the Lord in the Cameron Highlands. The way is therefore clear for us to go ahead and make precise arrangements....

To me this is a wonderful answer to prayer, for we were certainly faced with lions in the way. They have turned out to be chained ones and I believe you can go ahead in confidence that the Lord will continue to work on your behalf as you meet each difficulty in the days that lie unknown before you.

Very sincerely yours in Him
A J Broomhall

And none of us knew then that Chefoo School's Headmaster would be resigning the next year.

## Somebody Nobody

*Always, I wanted to be somebody.*
*At four, it was an accountant:*
*My uncle had his own office*
*With an adding up machine I'd use when he let*
*me*
*... And when he didn't let me but wasn't looking.*
*Then, after the Sunday School play,*
*It was acting.*
*I was going to have shows on television,*
*Star in films*
*And re-do all the Milky Bar Kid adverts.*
*By six, I was to be a boxer*
*So that I could clobber Jonathan Upton,*
*The police sergeant's son,*
*Who needed clobbering.*
*When I bashed him anyway*
*He keeled straight over.*

*But he got back up*
*And that was the start of my ambition to be a*
*runner.*
*I almost made it at cross-country*
*Cause no one else was stupid enough*
*To charge through mud every wet Wednesday.*
*After that ...*
*Goodness, I forget, there were so many ideas,*
*Each one making me a somebody.*
*Then you happen along, Lord,*
*And you say, "You're a nobody,"*
*Which I claim is oversimplified and offensive*
*And privately recognise is true.*
*So how come, Lord,*
*When I finally agree to be nobody,*
*I feel like somebody at last?*

*Dave Kitchen*

# 4

# A Brown Study

lothes packed; clothes to be packed; clothes to be
C ironed; clothes to be name-taped ... And trunks
— they spilled over from *Heatherlea's* small hallway,
cluttering the lounge and dining room. A miscellany
of the Miller Trio's moveables decorated every flat
surface and that wasn't the worst; there were things
called "decisions". What type of living accommoda-
tion would we have? Did we need a kettle? lamps?
blankets? When we pitched in to deal with plates,
pans and precious things, should we include, for
instance, our dinner service? Would we need it to
entertain the parents of "all those missionaries'
children"? They'd be sure to visit the school sometimes. The thing was — a missionary from Africa we
knew, had poured her china into the bin on her
return.

Ruth set up her sewing machine amid the para-
phernalia. Ruth was a member of our home Bible
study group but she was also a Home Economics
teacher. Her role in the move, to crown her skill at
running up cotton dresses, was the application of

Cash's name tapes to a few hundred articles. But which shirts of J-boy's should be named? Could we take his colourful checked outfits to a country where the teacher class was supposed to wear only white? Perhaps I'd better add "long-sleeved white shirts for Jonathan" to a shopping list which looked like Alice in Wonderland's puzzled idea of the mouse's "tale". And then, what about the hand luggage — such a limited amount? Wouldn't we need summery things among it because it was winter here and the tropics there?

What should I do with my elegant burgundy winter coat with its fashionable half-belt and sprung skirt? It was a new and stylish present from my mother to wear for our goodbye services. But it was Donegal tweed and that would be way too hot even in the mountains where the school was. Mini-lengths would be out by the time we saw *Heatherlea* again. Oh dear — was it a flash of self-knowledge that made me suddenly feel what I wanted most in life was to stay in Londonderry and wear it?

I'd better make a note to see my optician. If I lost a contact lens in the jungle, wouldn't I need glasses to revert to?

Would our passports arrive in time?

And *Heatherlea* itself. Perhaps this dear little house, in which we'd invested so much of our lives, was the most pressing problem of all. If we let it, would the tenants care for the precious things we left?

My arm was so sore. In fact, I was sure I had a fever and there were to be more inoculations next week.

I sat down in the middle of the muddle and cried.

Were we going to rue the day we ever decided to be missionaries? All my life I'd been used to doing my own thing. Supposing I didn't like Chefoo ... Suppos-

ing I didn't want to teach a class of missionaries' kids
... What then? Yet if God had "called" us, why should I
be bothered about whether I'd like it or not? Couldn't
I be content with the thought of being "a real
missionary" at last? But other missionaries I knew
were zealous dedicated people — people on pedestals,
spiritually-minded, doing the will of God whatever.
Was there such a thing ever, as another missionary
like me? A recruit who bounced forward at God's call
because that was what she thought was a good idea
anyway?

Maybe it wasn't a good idea after all. At that
moment my zest for adventure with God was at an
all-time low — that is, since I became really serious
about getting to know God. I'd never thought a flit to
the Far East would involve us all in such trauma.
*Heatherlea* painted a portrait of home, more than ever
before — the expression of eleven happy colourful
years of marriage — especially the little blue and
white nursery.

Not that *it* could stay as it was much longer
anyway, for J-boy had been barely five when he
informed me one day that Raymond, with whom he
played in the park, didn't call *his* bedroom a *nursery*.
Raymond had *brown* furniture. Raymond had wall-
paper with trains and motorbikes and aeroplanes on
it, not *teddy bears*. And Raymond's bed had a head-
board that was a grown-up one, *not* blue and white.
He sounded so disgusted with his lot in life that we'd
decided to make him a schoolboy's bedroom soon.

Now it would be in Malaysia — far away from
Raymond.

Far away, too from our own friends — the house
Bible study folk, the children in the Sunday School at
St Augustine's church, our teacher colleagues and our

neighbours like Florence who was so interested in our decision to be missionaries. Wouldn't we miss friends like George and Pat with whom we'd grown up? We were twin couples, who enjoyed matching our time-tables — whether going to college, deciding to become engaged, have a wedding or produce a baby son over four years later (a feat we'd managed within nine days of each other). Could we live without our families, especially Mum and Dad Rankin and Mr Miller, Senior?

Looking out of *Heatherlea's* picture window with its view of the huge hospital on Altnagelvin Hill, I saw that it was snowing — a flurry of tiny flakes reshaping the scene from the grey of winter to a dreamy Narnia-land. I loved the snow. Malaysia's mountains, almost on the earth's equator, would never see snow.

The morning-after this gloomy night-before was quite different. I am so glad that God created mornings. I've always been a morning person with an optimistic view of life when the day is young and a correspondingly low trough when I'm overtired in the evening after all my exertions. This has caused a few problems in our family because John is no lark. John is an owl. Mornings see John struggling to be with it through layers of somnolent fog. One Sunday, after he had burned the midnight oil getting his sermon to gel and I had had one of my exciting isn't-the-world-beautiful feelings at four am, we discovered we had only overlapped one hour in bed.

Anyway one day, one beautiful morning in March 1970, it was all over. The straw was hoovered off the carpets, the wardrobes were bare, the roof-space was jammed tight with memories, we'd returned from London where OMF had given us a Candidate Course, all our farewell services were in the past and the new

American tenants knew how to defrost the fridge. We even seemed to know how to dress for the flight.

Anticipation of the adventure was, by then, so absolute that we could say our goodbyes happily at Belfast's small airport. But, we didn't know that we'd never see dear Mr Miller again — in this life, that is; he, who was so involved in all we were doing; he, who never complained; a gentle Christian man with a world of reading in his mind. Mr Miller was the one who taught his skill of professional lettering to John; the one from whom J-boy inherited his artistic ability. This man, who had never been in hospital in his life, was to go to be with the Lord one Sunday morning during the church service — just three weeks after we left home, when the daffodils were blowing in the church graveyard.

I'm glad we didn't know as the plane taxied along the tarmac. I'm glad we didn't know either that we were leaving our special ones to a decade and more of terrorist activity in Northern Ireland, when murders and heinous atrocities would hit the headlines worldwide. No more would we return to gentle green hills and peaceful pastures. The Emerald Isle was to change vastly before we ever landed on her soil again.

Belfast, London, Brussels, Athens, Bombay, Bangkok and — Singapore.

Today's non-stop flights between London and Singapore make that first one seem like a marathon. It was Asian time when we arrived — midnight. The soft balmy humid air enveloped us as the cabin door opened. And there was OMF to greet us.

# Out of the Mouths of Babes

## Out of the Mouths of Babes

"What is a saint?" the teacher said.
With watchful eye and weary tread
She lead her charges round the church,
In archaeological research —
To most of her class a saint was dead!

"A saint is a person the light shines through,"
Said the smallest child, as she stood to view
A stained-glass window, wide and high,
Drawing shafts of sun from a cloudless sky,
A Joseph-coat brightness of rainbow hue.

The teacher smiled with happy surprise,
For no moral she might devise
Could describe more exactly the attribute "good"
Or be more perfectly understood
Than this truth of the ageless wise.

*She smiled again, for her words at last*
*Had reaped their reward for all the past*
*Lessons she thought fell on stony ground;*
*For, with joy, and thankfulness, now she found*
*A new awareness of knowledge held fast.*

*The child smiled too, with pleasure of praise,*
*And remembered the incident all her days,*
*For when she was older, and growing grey,*
*She said to her own grandchild one day,*
*"You will know the saints, and they will know*
*you*
*If they see the light of God's love shining*
*through."*

Stella M. Entwistle

# 5

# *Technicoloured Threshold*

W ay back in October 1962 when I awoke in the Bayview Nursing Home, Londonderry, after Jonathan's birth, morning was glory-gowned. Could it really be that I had a son? It was three am but despite sedatives I was far too excited to sleep again. I wanted to climb to the sky and shout to Londonderry that the nicest baby ever had just arrived and he was mine! I didn't, of course. I just asked for the draped cradle to be brought alongside my bed for him to captivate me completely.

It was with a thrill akin to this that I awoke in Singapore that first day in March 1970. Was this adventure really happening to me? We were meant to be sleeping late to compensate for jet lag, but I could hear the Chinese cooks down below haranguing in their tonal language. I could hear tropical birds in the garden. In fact, I could hear Singapore, its great island heart throbbing with all sorts of noises because we couldn't close our louvre windows in the excessive heat.

I admit I sometimes seem to have an overdose of

enthusiasm for life when I want to sing in tune with King David, "The boundary lines have fallen for me in pleasant places". During these highs in temperament, it seems such a waste of time to sleep. A pity! The troughs are all the lower afterwards. But the way Singapore affected me made me want to send cables to everyone at home to come and enjoy it all too. Of course, I didn't do that either. I have great enthusiasms but John has his size nine shoes firmly planted on Asian terra firma.

First days can be somewhat unpredictable. The Assistant General Director wanted to see us.

Wondering why, we proceeded as hastily as the humid heat would allow to Mr Lea's office. His sudden disclosure took us totally by surprise.

"I'll drop the bombshell right away", he started. "Mr Parker at Chefoo is leaving. Can you take up the principalship of the school in the New Year, John?"

Silently we tried to come to terms with what was involved. No village life in Malaysia after Language School so that we could become fluent in Malay and understand more fully the role of the missionary parent. Instead, after four months' study, we were to go straight to Chefoo to have a time of overlap with Mr Parker. Not only was Chefoo staffed by seven teachers, but also with dorm aunties, who cared for the children in out-of-school hours. Just then the school was short-staffed on the home side so that's where I was slotted in for six months.

"What do you feel about it all?" asked Mr Lea.

John accepted the challenge. So with excited exuberance we left the heat a few days later to settle Jonathan in Chefoo, looking forward to returning to the island where dreams come true and hearing what the Malay language sounded like.

The journey through Malaysia culminated in a forty-mile stretch of mountain road, snaking its way via five hundred bends to a plateau five thousand feet high called Tanah Rata. The sickening trip was compensated for fully when we rounded that last U-turn — the curve in Chefoo's driveway.

At last! After all those months of anticipation, there it was — the valley campus, peppered with blond children!

The driver manoeuvered his steering-wheel carefully, skirting the playing field, unaware of the sensations his backseat passengers were experiencing. Also unaware, a group of little girls sat in a circle on the grass by the drive, their long fair hair draping their faces like twin curtains. Chefoo was beautiful! It was as though the great Creator of hanging baskets had let one slip from His hook in the sky to nestle there among the mountains — especially for the small students who were to tenant that terrain in years to come. That afternoon the sun was shining. Leaving Chefoo in 1979, I still loved that valley.

But it was back to Singapore for us — without J-boy. He was in his new red Ladybird dressing-gown when we said goodbye, his red robin cheeks smudged with tears ... Despite the adventure of it all, I blew my nose frequently on the drive down the mountain.

Back to temperatures in the nineties, back to mosquitoes whose bites left oozing blisters any place where they could syphon off Irish blood, back to geckos scuttling over walls and ceilings forcing me to have my Bible readings under the mosquito net lest one would miss its footing, and — back to LANGUAGE STUDY.

The study hours were long — six per day just on Malay. We dropped all the clangers common to language learners everywhere. One day, in an effort to start conversing, our teacher said, "Now, Mrs Sheila, what did you do on Saturday?"

"I went and had my grass cut," I explained fluently.

"Oh? Where did you do that?"

"At the grass-cutting salon."

"Do you mean, Mrs Sheila, that you had your hair cut?"

"Oh!" I gasped in confusion and English, "your words 'rumput' and 'rambut' are so alike!"

"Yes, I understand," smiled Cik Tutik, whom we liked immensely, "just like your words 'chicken' and 'kitchen'."

I'd never thought of that before!

The language learning group was truly international. They had joined us from various ends of the earth and were heading towards a variety of East Asian countries, majoring in whatever language was required. Despite the ache of longing for Jonathan, I found life assuming the joy of a long Christian Conference.

Bart and Margaret headed up the course. Brian and Lois came with their superb slides of New Zealand, Doug and Margie from the States. Graham and Heather, who often scurried from the dining room with a howling two-year-old, hailed from England. Among lots of others were Bong and Alma, the latter playing volleyball so enthusiastically that her fashionable wig fell off. Without turning a hair (of her own), Alma, an American Chinese, picked it up, set it in place once more and resumed play.

It was Alma, too, who dashed to the centre of the front row to volley the next ball. It just so happened that John was in the front line of attack also — at the other side. He had the same notion about playing the shot. Collision. Literally they fell into each other's arms. Someone chose that moment to call the score. "Love all"!

It is unfortunate if a missionary-to-be comes into this world with an unadventurous palate. Living in the Far East brought us face to face with some incredible edibles. The policy of Language Centre was to accustom us to a variety of these before we would leave Singapore. John and I both found lunchtime an hour to rejoice if the table wasn't set with chopsticks. Chinese take-aways hadn't reached Ireland when we were growing up so delicacies such as shark's fin soup only slithered down to be recalled in flavour for days to follow.

The fruit durian, highly prized by Chinese, was another gastronomical experience. Some of our group thought it tasted okay if you could get past its smell. I couldn't help remembering J-boy's disgust when once I had served my two-year-old with a new recipe in Heatherlea. "What *is* this, Mummy? It tastes terbibble. It is *bestremely* not nice!" And then, to complicate matters, I became allergic to prawns. However, to put us at ease a charming Asian dentist, having listened to our excuses for not wanting a second helping of seafood one evening at a restaurant on the coast, said, "I quite understand. Don't worry a thing about it. As for myself, I can't get potatoes past my throat."

Despite these idiosyncracies, I have wonderful memories of that four months in Chancery Lane, Singapore, in the building that is now the Discipleship Training Centre. Soon we could chat in simple Malay. We greatly appreciated all that OMF stood for as we learned more about it. We jostled with tourists buying batik cloth at Singapore's night markets. We visited a rubber plantation and saw something of Hinduism, Buddhism and Islam.

We explored Change Alley and learned about Sir Stamford Raffles. We taught in St Hilda's Church — John melting in a white cassock and surplice and I sweating it out in a fanless classroom. We smelt smells that had never wafted across our paths before, like the fragrance of frangipani and the whiff from the hawkers' stalls. We witnessed monsoon drains like roofless railway tunnels gushing with torrential rain, and heard the drumming to keep evil spirits away at a Chinese funeral.

But even though I treasure all these thoughts, I know there were times of mental exhaustion, of inertia and a definite lack of the euphoric state.

One day the mission arranged for our group to have some hours of prayer. The special speaker was to be Mr Ernie Heimbach, one of OMF's directors from the States.

In the big meeting room the fans whirred lazily, stirring the hot air. Yet as Mr Heimbach began to draw word pictures of his missionary life in Thailand, the stifling atmosphere seemed to recede and I was alive and with him on the mountain trails. So graphic was his message, that he, too, left the picture and Sheila Miller was alone in her seat with God.

I thought, *Well, that's what it means to be a real missionary. I could never go to tribesland. I'd positively hate it. All that hardship. How ghastly. You have to give up so much to be that kind of missionary. But me, I haven't given up anything to go to Chefoo. It's something I've wanted to do and I'll love it.*

"What if you exchange your short-term appointment for a commitment for life?" a still small Voice whispered in my heart.

*But*, I argued, *everything is working out so nicely as it is. When we have our associate membership finished, Jonathan will be eleven. That's the limit of Chefoo's education for him. We'll take him back home for his secondary education in 1974.*

"What if you change your minds?"

I began to feel alarmed. Were these thoughts perhaps God's Voice? Was this yet another idea, an unenthusiastic one for a change, that I'd have to identify as the Lord's?

But ... *boarding school for Jonathan?*

"Lord," I whispered, "I know other missionaries cope with that, even when their little children are only six years old. But, Father, *Jonathan?* Lord, we only have one child. He doesn't have a sister who could keep me company if he went home. There wouldn't be a brother to take my mind off his absence. It couldn't be right for *our* family."

Or could it?

The tropical sun slanted across the room, its light catching the tear drops falling off my chin onto the open Bible. I was crying because I knew that morning that our commitment to God could never be short term. And I was crying, too, because I realized I might never be able to wash J-boy's rugby gear. In days to come it seemed the epitome of despair that I might never get the chance.

Yes, if we returned to Chefoo after a leave, it would be a sacrifice then all right. That day I couldn't quite see how we could face it but I knew then it was on the cards.

That prayer-day, as the shadows indicated evening, John began to talk. I'd never heard him mention anything like this before.

"You know, Sheila," he said, "until today, I

haven't ever felt I could send Jonathan to boarding school."

How could it be that on this very evening John should introduce a conversation about the possibility of separation in our family? Mr Heimbach's talk had been about the fishermen caught in a storm on the lake. He had pointed out that God doesn't exempt his disciples from difficulties and, yes, he had said that obedience involves risk. Was this what had sparked off our mutual thought patterns?

"Is it right to expect anyone else to bring up *our* son the way we would like?" John went on. "As I was thinking about it, God seemed to be drawing my attention to Hannah and Samuel. That mother left *her* little boy at the temple and went back to Ramah without him. She left him with an old man who couldn't even bring up his own sons. Yet look how it worked out for the glory of God. Sheila," John ended, "I have confidence for the first time about possibly leaving Jonathan at home in years to come if it is right for our family; if Jonathan could take it."

That prayer day, with its tears, seemed to draw aside Heaven's curtains just a fraction for us. We both realized that adventure with God was a thrilling thing in the halcyon now but — what would happen when the honeymoon years were over?

# Chefoo

Children playing in the grass,
    A euphony of sight and sound,
A sweet commingled shade so bright
    The tune of laughter floating round.
Though homes are far away, it's true
Children are happy at Chefoo.

Children sitting still in class,
    Quiescence rare, yet so worthwhile,
For minds stretch now and research brings
    The sought-for knowledge to each file.
There's not one thing I'd rather do
Than teach the children at Chefoo.

Children walking down to church,
    Clean fresh shirts and dresses new,
Where are Timmy, Anne and Jayne?
    Their blonde-combed hair I hardly knew.
Behaviour, too, within the pew
Isn't the normal for Chefoo!

Children sleeping in the dorm,
    A quiet hush pervades the air
Which was so recently the scene
    Of bedtime games, stories and prayer.
But now small forms and faces strew
The crumpled beds here at Chefoo.

A school, a home, inseparable,
    Enormous family with one link -
Here for Mum and Dad have gone
    To preach the gospel. Don't you think
They need our prayers? God counts on you
To pray for the children at Chefoo.

Sheila Miller

# 6

# *How green was our valley*

"**M**ummy, you've made a dreadful mistake!" It was our seven-year-old bouncing in from his next-door dorm. I followed his gaze. The door from our bedsit into my dormitory lay open. "Aunty Ann never," he exploded, "never lets us make a mess of our beds like that!"

Jonathan was deciding then that his mother just didn't know anything. With an airy wave of his hand, he concluded that my ten "middle-aged" girls were being dis-cooperative. "Dis-cooperative" was a new word I'd learned in Singapore from Jonathan's bed-time prayer confessions.

Despite Jonathan's fears that discipline in the school was about to crumble, no hint of bedlam surfaced with my new family. Six months later when life began for me in a Chefoo classroom, I found the same innocuous demeanour — rather rare for the seventies. Being tucked away from the world in Malaysia's jungle was doing things for our kids. I began to be glad that J-boy wasn't having his primary schooling at home. Besides, reports of life in Northern

Ireland were beginning to filter through. Disturbing tales of riots and turmoil.

It was midnight in the jungle when I first braved the arrival of my own Chefusians — one weekend in August, 1970.

They were filthy!

I felt as if I was involved in Child Welfare and had picked them off the streets. No way could I scrub the dirt out of Evvie's toenails. She'd hiked for two days down a muddy mountain trail before she could even start her real journey to Chefoo. At that stage a flight flung her from North Thailand to Bangkok where she caught a train bound for Malaysia, with sixty others en route for the school in the jungle.

Evvie ate on that train, slept there and tackled brush ups. She pencilled a letter to her parents back in North Thailand as hour after tiring hour the train sped further from her tribesland home. Chefoo staff mopped away tears, produced comics, games, crayons; chatted and mothered; fed, watered and tucked up their small travellers until, near nightfall next day, in the steamy heat of the border town, they resumed their marathon in taxis.

For six hours they huddled in the dark, weaving along Malaysia's highways until the mountain road to Chefoo began to twist in a forty-mile spiral ascent to the plateau at the top.

Evvie had made it and that first Saturday was different from anything I'd ever experienced in my life before. Unpacking ten trunks. Shampooing seven blonde heads, two dark and one red. Cutting two hundred nails. Supervising play. And with it all, building bridges. At eight o'clock when our valley's greenness was screened by night, I thrust them between their clean sheets and — I *had had* it.

But they were precious. They were natural.

"Aunty Sheila, did you know that we have a very special little brother in our family?" It was later I discovered he was a Down's baby.

"Aunty Sheila, do you know what we did in school today? We learned all about the nabertackle"!

*Perhaps,* I thought, *I'll be a dorm aunty for ever and not a teacher at all!* Yet when the New Year dawned I was delighted to switch to familiar territory — the classroom.

Teaching at Chefoo! So like the daily Irish routine of the past yet how dissimilar. A classroom is a classroom anywhere with its charts, pictures and projects pinned to the bulletin boards. On the roster, the same 3 Rs prevailed plus plenty of novel variations. But ... these children found themselves on this mountain top, having scaled it from all over planet earth. Americans and British. Australians and New Zealanders. South Africans and Europeans. International. Like a summit talk or the Olympic Games.

Dollars and cents. Pounds and pence. T-r-a-v-e-l-e-r and t-r-a-v-e-l-l-e-r. P-l-o-w and p-l-o-u-g-h. Laura Ingalls Wilder *and* Noel Streatfield. Senate *and* Parliament. The Rockies *and* the Pennines — not to mention the Blue Mountains, the South African Table and the Swiss Alps.

Or was the differing dimension the quality of the kids? No dis-cooperation. One little girl did seem to have learning problems. I curbed my impatience at the slow way her mind grasped new concepts compared with her peers. At the end of the school year, I was rather taken aback. She scored 100 in her IQ test. 100 is average. She wasn't dim after all. It was just that the others were incredibly sharp.

Once, though, what-was-thought-to-be-thenaughtiest-thing-ever happened. A family arrived back from home leave brimful of a choice new language which was definitely not acceptable at Chefoo! They'd picked it up at school in England's industrial north. To boot, their rough-ups began to spill over into classroom, dormitory and playground.

One by one the staff came to John with this news.

"All right," said John, "I'll see them."

The three diminutive culprits stood unabashed before his office desk.

"Can you guess why I sent for you?" asked John.

Silence. They couldn't.

"Well, I'll go on writing my letter while you think it over."

After several minutes he raised his head. "Have you thought of a reason yet?"

Blank stares. There just wasn't anything they could ever have done wrong.

"Take some time longer to think," suggested John. "I haven't finished my letter."

At last a small voice piped up. Carefully avoiding its slum smut, it asked in good evangelical jargon, "Is it that we are not having good fellowship with our friends?" One of the rare occasions when three small posteriors felt as though they had been sunburnt!

John was seldom required to be a disciplinarian yet his new post was a tremendous challenge. Of all the tasks that fell to his lot, running the gamut from killing poisonous snakes to hiring a new gardener, the one he loved most was leading morning assembly. Creatively he would search around in his mind for new ideas to present the Christian faith to these open-hearted children. Each week day we had a different half-hour programme. Criss Cross Quiz, Jungle Doctor Stories with puppets or Whiteboard talks; Tuesday Tune Time and Friday Filmstrip; Interviews, Overhead Projector Serials and Drama.

Acting! Those mornings stand out to be counted! We were studying the parables of the Lord Jesus. One day we settled down to view a child walk on the stage — no, a university student enter a second-hand bookshop. Far from our reckoning was the thought of this little scene having a sequel — comic or tragic (depending where you were standing in the wings).

In this scene the small scholar perched on a ladder browsing through academic-looking tomes. But what was this? A paper fluttered to the floor. I still have it here as I write:

"Date: Centuries ago

Dear Reader of this book,
This is the original owner of the book writing to you. You must have been reading this book very carefully to find these hidden words. You obviously love books. I too loved books and I want this book and all my riches to go into your hands. Buy this book and you won't regret it — no matter how much it costs you. Make sure that whatever else you do, you become the owner of this book.
Signed: The original owner."

But the book was costly — secondhand bookshop though it was. The child-student replaced it furtively, carefully hiding it at the back of the shelf. And the next scene saw him selling his cassette recorder, his guitar, his bicycle; anything to find enough cash to purchase his prize.

An animated movement stirred the watching children. Their friend was back in the shop. He was counting out his money. Enough! The book was his!

Was it worth it? Of course! A roll of ten dollar

Malay notes fell from the spine!

And a hush descended on the small listeners as John stood to read the words of the Lord Jesus from St Matthew's gospel, "The kingdom of heaven is like treasure hidden in a field. When a man found it, he hid it again, and then in his joy went and sold all he had and bought that field ...."

Come the end of that month, John's secretary, Kar Yong, appeared in his office with a furrowed brow and the school accounts file. She was having difficulty balancing the books. John, mathematically minded, lost no time going into every detail of the statistics presented. But in no way could he match the expenditure with the money in hand. The cash box was several hundred Malay dollars short.

However, a few days later Kar Yong said that everything had sorted itself out and John forgot the incident.

Months passed.

Then one night, for, being an owl, John was having his devotional time late, he found it necessary to check out a verse in his Thompson Chain Reference Bible — a large, heavy hard-backed edition!

Into his lap tumbled hundreds of Malay dollars.

The treasure in the field! It had been this big heavy Bible John had used to hide the money in the play. Had he or the child pushed the notes back into their hiding place? He couldn't remember. Then, in consternation, he recalled Kar Yong's problems with the school accounts. No wonder! The school cash-box was where the money had come from in the first place!

Next morning he discovered that Kar Yong had made up the deficiency from her own purse. So not only the children learned a lesson from the parable!

Chefoo terms go on and on. And on. Sometimes stretching as far as nineteen weeks! But only two per year, each separated by a long family holiday. This way the children aren't subject to difficult travel too often.

However the term is amply peppered with good things including a week-long half-term's activities. As a teacher I found that week more demanding than any other. I was like a warrior insufficiently armoured for the fray.

The fray involved water fights, cross-country runs and swimming galas. It included progressive suppers and back-to-front days (when you started the morning with a hot bath and ended the day with breakfast). Once a Chefoo Fair was dreamed up by some dorm aunty, quite out of her depth with enthusiasm. That was when the principal had to poke his head through a hole which immediately turned him into Aunt Sally and the target for over-ripe tomatoes. Then there came the Chefoo Circus for we had a tremendous conglomeration of pets. Tiny Glyn made a terrific lion-tamer, tugging along Tiger Lily, the newest kitten, in a hamster cage. Spot-The-Staff-Member-Day meant we had to disguise ourselves in outrageous outfits. Imagine sixteen of us scattered round the green campus waiting to be recognized — sudden desperate window-cleaners, extra Bourneville-coloured gardeners, superfluous patients in Sick Bay under the blankets plus many another hilarious camouflage to mystify the kids. One little auburn-haired beauty came upon me strategically standing just round the corner of the cottage, hands held high. In a panic, she dashed away from my charismatic pose, yelling, "I-I-s-s-saw a *ghost* — pretending to be Aunty Sheila."

Perhaps the cook outs were most special of all. New things like shish kebabs, dilly-dogs and dough boys were poked into braziers under a denim sky. The holiday atmosphere was contagious. Eating a grizzled sausage, I found myself chatting to a new father. He'd brought his little pre-schooler to the Camerons. The purpose wasn't so much for holiday but the need to assess Chefoo. Would the school — this *boarding* school — be right for *his* family? He sat there on the step outside Dorm 2 and in between munches he confided, "Arriving at Chefoo I feel as though I've died, and wakened up in heaven."

One half-term evening we watched the tropical night close in down by the stream. Chefoo's stream lay low in the valley with gently sloping banks on either side. It was a natural amphitheatre — just the place for a camp fire singalong. John led us till our throats were hoarse in "Alice where art thou going?" or "John Brown's motor has a puncture in its tyre" or "I took my dear old mother-in-law...." There seemed to be no end to the "come-all-ye's" John remembered from his Scouting days. It was fun for me to recall how often he had regaled my mother from the back seat of their picnic-bound car, to Ralph Reader's mother-in-law song. The words were choice.

"I took my dear old mother-in-law
A-bathing in the ocean
The way she kicked and splashed about
She made a great commotion.
And how I laughed, 'Ha-ha, ha-ha',
And oh, how I gloated
For one of her legs was made of cork
And the wrong way up she floated."!

Darkness was shrouding the valley when we rose from the dying embers to proceed bedwards. It had been a good day. But an elderly couple who had joined us for the fun of the evening approached the brand new headmaster as he unfolded himself from scattering sand on the ashes. "Mr Miller," the missionary lady began, "do you ever teach them any little Christian choruses?"

One innovation that New Year was the introduction of Clubs in out-of-school hours. Ideas? The staff was full of them — anything from photography for the older boys to Teddy bears' picnics for the little ones. The new Cub-Scout Troop sang out "Akela, we'll do our best," till the mountains echoed. The senior girls began to appear in newly-crocheted ponchos and, ever since, the poncho has been a high fashion favourite there, under "the enchanted canopy", as the world's rain forests have been called. Clubs for the athletic, clubs for the crafty. Clubs for — the staff! Elvira demonstrated how to make candles. Em taught us macrame. Barry endured our attempts at guitar strumming.

So what with sports day, class parties, the school play; what with Christmas celebrations starting in November, class assemblies and soccer matches, there was always something to look forward to. No wonder David Pawson of the Millmead Centre, Guildford, England said after a visit, "I'm sure this must be the happiest school in the world."

I don't mean there were no tears. Of course we cried. Of course we were homesick and ordinary-sick too. Once a flu epidemic attacked seventy of us in its spate. Our dear old pony, Pete, died — the one that Ned, our American "dorm-uncle", had dressed up and led on to the stage at one morning assembly, showing the children how to handle him. In fact, old Pete's replacement died too. He was a beautiful chestnut bought in the holidays to surprise the Chefusians on their return. What hours of enjoyment they would have! But before ever Lord Chester gave one ride, he slipped in the stream. Nothing could mend that damaged joint. He was laid to rest in Chester's Field.

Our snowy angora bunnies were attacked by wild dogs from the village. Only white puffs of fluff on the playing field next morning told the story. Georgina, Ned's otter, fell off the balcony, and as her mate had already disappeared down a monsoon drain in Kuala Lumpur almost as soon as he was bought, we weren't able to raise baby otters after all. The goats had to go too, and their kids — the ones we'd watched being born in that natural amphitheatre down by the stream. But they ate everything in sight including the gardener's roses.

Tears dampened pillow slips many a night, but morning light often shone through the drops, refracting colour. Sibelius once said of his music that it was as if the Almighty had thrown pieces of mosaic down from heaven's floor and it was his business to put them together again. Chefoo's children were fragments of mosaic given to us by the Lord — beautiful, irridescent and together they made life in that faraway valley a colourful whole.

# A Highland Testimony

We had our ritual too. Down the long glen,
While startled curlews cried on ebb-tide sands,
We all would walk, our Bibles in our hands,
And winter sunshine turned to rain again.

The crisp and cutting edge of our dark suits
Served as a weekly penance. We, in turn,
Would kick some chuckies into ditch or burn,
And scuff the polish on our Sunday boots.

The church bell spread its iron news abroad,
Dull through the trees or clear across the bay.
With quickened step we hastened on our way.
And so we entered in the house of God.

Thus went the ritual of that far-off day.
The creak of bell and bell-rope clanged and jarred.
The psalms were dignified. The pews were hard.
The rain was soft. The lowering skies were grey.

Grey too the tenour of our world today.
The death of humanism, sick and sad.
And I could wish that once again we had
That child's acceptance of the Christian way.

Faith of my fathers. If it came again,
I would not change a moment of my youth,
The grey kirk and the straight unflinching truth,
Clean as the stones at the burn-side in the glen.

*Alistair Halden*

# 7

# Red Sails in the Sunset

Long before I'd ever heard of Chefoo; before life in the Far East was a reality, I was delighting in the knowledge that I had reached my twenties. Grown-up at last! I'd graduated from college in Belfast and by the time I was 22, I was wearing John's platinum ring. John found me just when I was experiencing something new in Christianity: my blinkers were beginning to slip. (Or, as the Americans on the Chefoo staff would say, the blinders began to fall off of me!) These blinkers had been firmly fixed in place by my Northern Irish culture. They had shuttered my spiritual perspective for years, screening me from real Christianity. As the removal began, I glimpsed a vista — vast and more precious than my diamonds.

Northern Ireland is staunchly Christian. I was born hearing the gospel of the Saviour. As a small girl, I accompanied my parents to meeting after evangelistic meeting. Could there ever have been a date when I didn't realize that human beings come into the world sinful from birth? I needed to be reborn. I knew that, little as I was. Reborn into God's family.

A warm and beautiful something responded inside me to all this teaching. God loved me! That was special. And I loved back. The instruction fired at me was like priming a stove. My response to the love of the Lord Jesus was instant ignition.

One early transaction tooled itself on my memory in gold. I was seven. The curtain was rising for the next scene in my young life — over Portstewart. World World II had started. Londonderry was a strategic port. The wail of air-raid sirens became too familiar. Night after night, closeted by blackness, my mother had the three of us children, Sheila, Terence and Adeline, tiptoe down from our beds to "under the stairs".

This was adventure. Mum had taken out the cleaning things, the buckets and whatever. In there she'd put a picnic table and as the bombs dropped we drank fizzy lemonade. I don't remember ever being afraid although, surely, *she* must have been. Dad was out patrolling, checking that everyone's blackout blinds were effective.

One morning the neighbours were agog with the news that last night's blast had blown out a window in No. 11. That was when Dad and Mum decided on evacuation. We left our big terrace house and moved to Portstewart for a year. Portstewart is a charming seaside town where Ireland's north coast meets the Atlantic Ocean.

Holiday days in Portstewart were extra special. Sitting on the huge stone steps leading down to the sea, I was one of the general mêlée at the beach mission. I usually had to take my little sister with me and *she* had to take her teddy bear. There we sat in this natural theatre clad in our war-time liberty bodices under our "frocks", our Clark's sandals, and our hair tied in a big bunch to one side with a huge ribbon apiece.

"Sheila," my mother said one morning, "Adeline has lost her teddy bear. Ask the man after the meeting if it turned up yesterday."

The "announcements" were the highlight of these mornings with invitations to sausage sizzles, sand hockey, race-the-tide competitions, sand-castle-building and a finale of a lost property list! The young fellow up front was having a ball. "...an umbrella, two Bibles, several cardigans and — a *teddy bear*." The audience, sprinkled liberally with fond adults, howled in amusement. But I was mesmerized. No *way* would my muscles function to claim Adeline's teddy. No way could I endure that embarrassment! I never ever heard what happened to it!

The backdrop to this theatre was the setting which inspired the lyric "Red Sails in the Sunset" but after the message, the appeal was that we children should sing, not the old nostalgic song, but one that was even more apposite, "Come into my heart Lord Jesus. Come in today, come in to stay."

The gold tooling took place as again my young heart surrendered. I asked the Lord Jesus to forgive my sins. Again I invited Him to live in my life. Somewhere along the line I later learned that one request is enough! He forgives and enters our lives at the first time of asking.

I've always loved Portstewart.

Yet Northern Ireland's Christianity lacked sunshine. It had local distinctives. I guess these idiosyncracies occur the world over. Dad used to tell how, in his youth, a young Christian seen with a tennis racquet was labelled "backslider". But at sweet sixteen I could play tennis without frowns of disapproval.

Nevertheless, a list of taboos was still there, with the "picture palace" right at the top. (A few decades later, TV brought those same films into Christian homes. Mind you, legalists still remarked, with reference to the skyward-pointing antennae, "I knew the devil was here. I saw his horns sticking out the chimney.")

But the Irish have strong feelings. We can plunge in right over our ears on issues like knitting, swimming or buying newspapers on Sundays; dancing, going to soccer matches or wearing make-up. More understandably, the abuse of alcohol meant a hardline stance on social drinking. Smoking, of course, was *out*, too.

Instead of casting our lot in with these worldly standards, we dutifully attended "meetings". On Sunday the members of our family were pentathletes: two services in the morning, one afternoon session and two more venues in the evening. But I did learn to read my Bible every day and, despite the negativism here and there, I am glad, really glad for positives; especially this one great fact: I, Sheila Patricia Rankin, was born in a Christian land, into a Christian family, to parents who made sure I knew about the Lord Jesus.

Singapore, where we now live, is an island of high-rise buildings. Walking down Orchard Road, feeling like a grease-blob, you can be constantly aware of the thump, thump, thump of a pile-driver. The nature of Singapore's soil makes pile-driving essential to ensure a good foundation for the newest skyscraper.

The positives in my background are stressed in my life like the bang of that pile-driving machine. Living in the Far East, I am aware more than ever of the blessings that were mine in Northern Ireland. No amount of dissonance can take that from me.

I don't think I ever knew that our particular brand of Christianity was a shade narrow. I'd nothing with which to compare it. Nothing, that is, until Mr and Mrs Roworth, Jonathan's godparents-to-be, dropped into Londonderry from Scotland. It was then that the blinkers began to make their exit.

Mr and Mrs Roworth's arrival was like adding a wide-angle lens to my spiritual camera. The panorama of their Christian thinking left me avid for the absolute arena. The longing was like trying to take in both the Horseshoe and American Falls at Niagara in one snapshot.

One evening Mrs Roworth was preparing supper in her up-to-date kitchen. I was idly waiting in the contemporary lounge with friends. From time to time I'd twist the new ring on my finger, just to see the diamonds sparkle. For a girl who had read *Pride and Prejudice* three times and who was looking for a Mr Darcy, my romance with John was sublimely low-key. We met in next-door classrooms. In an exciting environment like that, all you need to say is, "How do *you* go about introducing fractions to ten-year-olds?" Moonlight and roses were absent somehow. Nevertheless as John's intensely blue eyes found my brown gaze, the tingly joy of falling in love mingled amorously with the atmosphere of chalk dust!

Anyway, there I was, considering my gifts didn't lie in the kitchen (a problem with which John has had to live), when a hand touched my shoulder. Mrs R had come back on stage. The next few moments of drama were to radically change my lifestyle.

"Have you seen this, Sheila?" she asked. "It's OMF's newest book. Have a look. See what you think of it."

Thirty years later *By Searching* by Isobel Kuhn is still an OMF best-seller. In my youthful guilelessness, though, it was far from my mind that Mrs R was slipping into my hands a slab of paper dynamite. Rather passively, I opened *By Searching* at page one.

Now, if you really want to get through to me, there are three tentative tactics to try:

talk about John or Jonathan (appreciatively of course),

play a soul-stirring serenade, like "The Shepherd's Hymn after the Storm" in Beethovan's Pastoral Symphony or even "The Day I Met Marie" by my favourite rock 'n roll star, Cliff Richard (as I reckon I was preprogrammed at birth for rhythm!) and

read an emotive poem.

Isobel Kuhn had brought the latter into play.

I don't remember just then getting any further than that poem, even though its words were almost medieval. They exploded in my mind; they sneaked past all my defences for, as J B Phillips would have said, they were "shaped cunningly":

"To every man there openeth
A way and ways and a way.
And the high soul climbs the high way
And the low soul gropes the low
*And in between on the misty flats*
*The rest drift to and fro.*
But to every man there openeth
A high way and a low
And every man decideth the way
His soul shall go."

(John Oxenham)

Misty flats. Misty flats of Christian living.
Was that where I was? Drifting?
John Oxenham's thoughts wouldn't let me go. All

my life I hadn't been groping a low way but I couldn't claim I'd found a "high way" either.

I think I knew that evening that a climbing adventure with God was just around the corner for me. At last I began to need spiritual mountaineering boots.

College days in Belfast were just behind me. As a student, my life with God had been a slow saunter round the foothills of the highway He had planned for me. The flats there had been grey with mist. My peers had been enjoying "the world" and I actually got to thinking, "Now it would be nice to be a Christian later in life *after* I've had all the fun they're having."

But the timid side of me wouldn't let me join in with them, though I'd like to have done that. The Five Six Eight Club beckoned on Thursday nights, but then I'd been taught that a Christian shouldn't dance. I dated with various boyfriends who didn't know the Lord. Once during a home visit, my mother said to me, "Sheila, I don't know what's happened to you. You used to have such personality as a child. I never knew anyone who said the funny things you did! Why, when you were two, you met our maid at the door and told her, 'My mummy says you're no good. You never polish the step behind the kitchen door.' I just about died. And now, look at you. Why, you're an absolute *mouse*."

Well, the mouse in me kept me from exhaling great smoky gusts in my friends' faces and from flicking ash off a cigarette with a careless finger, with my stiletto heel cocked in an imitation of theirs; the mouse kept me from joining the rock and roll groups; kept me from falling too far ... The mouse? Well, perhaps it was The Hound. Francis Thompson's Hound of Heaven.

"I fled Him, down the nights and down the days;
  I fled Him, down the arches of the years;
  I fled Him, down the labyrinthine ways
Of my own mind; and in the mist of tears
I hid from Him, and under running laughter.
        Up vistaed hopes I sped;
        And shot, precipitated,
Adown Titanic glooms of chasmed fears,
From those strong Feet that followed, followed after.
        But with unhurrying chase,
        And unperturbed pace,
Deliberate speed, majestic instancy,
        They beat — and a Voice beat
        More instant than the Feet —
'All things betray thee, who betrayest Me.'

I had remained true to my cultural background yet during those college years I had also fled from the Hound of Heaven.

And that's how I got on to the misty flats.

It was while I was still climbing off them that the Miller Trio descended on Chefoo School, Malaysia. Pretty soon I discovered that Chefoo School was more than a school for missionaries' children. It was a school for adults as well. A zoom lens added itself to my wide-angle perspective. My heavenly camera began to focus more accurately on the lovely Person of the Lord Jesus. It seemed as if for years I had been marginally converted. The seventeenth century hymn writer, Johann Scheffler, had summed up my college Christianity succinctly when he wrote,
        "In darkness willingly I strayed,
            I sought Thee, yet from Thee I roved,
        Far wide my wandering thoughts were spread,

Thy creatures more than Thee I loved ..."
Now at Chefoo I discovered the reality in the couplet ending this verse,

"And now if more at length I see,
'Tis from Thy light and comes from Thee."

For years I'd missed the centre. Because of our contacts in our early married lives with dear Mr and Mrs Roworth, I had begun to emerge from my myopic mists and now, at last, it was the halfway house days that became blurred instead. Chefoo was high in the mountains but we scaled the heights in a taxi. As I rode out the loops on that first ascent, I had little inkling of the spiritual peaks ahead. They were to keep me greasing those mountaineering boots pretty often.

# Offering

Pulsating through each vein throbs vibrant life —
  rich vitality. Spirits high
    I reach for heaven.
      Bright, light-hearted praise
      Lilts skyward.

  And I
    find fond facility in song, and would
    join nature's bonds. My merry mood
    makes good —
  chants praises plural. So my voice I raise
      at little price.

Not ever will my temperament ascend
  to steeple heights. What when comes cloud,
    despondency and disposition's graph
      curves downwards?

  I'd vowed
            to praise my God. But what if
            disinclined?
            What tethered thought can set the
            mind?
            Rich find!
    that praise is noun and verb, a cenotaph,
            a sacrifice.

Sheila Miller

# 8

# *Colour It Radiant*

Cynthia lived at Chefoo. She was the Level 3 teacher — Jonathan's in fact. The difference in Cynthia's life and mine was striking. Cynthia did things like setting a rose in the bed-sit of a staff member who was particularly awkward. Cynthia gave her Saturdays to befriend someone feeling lonely in a valley with one road out, going almost nowhere. Cynthia saw positive things in people who set my teeth on edge.

And also there were Jenny, Em, Betty, Margie and a host of others — all like Cynthia. From Canada, England, Australia or wherever, dropped into this high-level valley by a God who knew we'd have to get on together. Roses in rooms whose occupant tried my patience? Doing something nice for someone I didn't like? I'd never heard of it. (I'm not sure where my thoughts were when I was reading the Bible!) I was so impressed that I made it the theme for the little story I wrote for children, *I Went to School in the Jungle*.

Books had always been a bonus in my life. Now somehow I got my hands on a little classic, *The Practice of the Presence of God* by Brother Lawrence. Was it the title attracted me? Was it this longing that had been there since childhood to respond to God, to know more, to oil my mountaineering boots? Only I kept getting in the way. Anyway what this French monk had to say to me three hundred years after he wrote it, penetrated some more of the fog that had smothered me for so long. His theme was his delight in experiencing God's presence in his kitchen — an unfeigned overwhelming delight. His thoughts high-lighted a void in my own life. I lacked that awareness of God he was talking about.

Basically I didn't know *how* to "practise the presence of God." After my morning Bible readings, I was inclined to lose track of God until bedtime or the next morning. My life was a dichotomy. A devotional part of me met the Lord most mornings and an intensely active me kept trying to achieve all day long — unrealistic goals of "doing" that left little time for "being" during the day, with my Saviour.

Brother Lawrence said, "Get the habit (good word for a monk) of entertaining yourself with God." He added, "... think often on God, by day, by night, in your business, and even in your diversions." Brother Lawrence wrote, "... a little remembrance of Him from time to time; a little adoration ... " and (as he advised the recipient of his letters), "Let him think of God the most he can. Let him accustom himself by degrees, to this small but holy exercise. No one will notice it and nothing is easier than to repeat often in the day these little internal adorations."

These ideas ice-axed the frozen sea inside me as Franz Kafka said good words should. While still living in Ireland, I had known a similar quiver of feeling somewhere deep within to Jean Rees' book *God*

*Wondered.* The Malays consider the seat of the emotions to be the liver. Something, my liver, my heart or whatever, responded. She had suggested that a housewife could use her chores as stimuli to prayer. As you make your son's bed, pray for the little scamp who sleeps in it. Sometimes when I'd be ironing my tea towels — a colour-fading-fast collection from all over the world — I'd mention to God the name of the friend who gave each. But the Chefoo classroom was a think-tank already. I was absorbed in "my" children, my teaching, more so than in my Heatherlea chores, so my precious Saviour was nudged to the side in all my busyness. I had no idea how to say, "Move over, Mary, Martha wants to sit down too."

I decided on a practical method to change me. After midday in the classroom, when the school bell joyfully jangled announcing lunch, I would deliberately pause at my desk as the children spilled on to the playground. The bell was to be a clanging reminder to me to recall during the day that I belonged to God and He was the God who was there; there in the Chefoo classroom. I would say a little prayer, I decided, before going for my own lunch.

The Psalmist wrote, "Seven times a day I praise you..."; my small total soared to two.

This mustard seed-size effort began to multiply. A new resolve was inching into my daily routine — to pause and remind myself that God was God Available; God Accessible. The habit wasn't totally prompted by feelings. It was something I had to *make* myself do if I wanted to change. Strange, that by forcing myself to act, I discovered shortly that it became natural for me to do that and I didn't need the school bell any longer.

The school bell. Chefoo. The Cameron Highlands.

That was a decade and more ago. Over the years a new awareness has dawned. The Lord has shown me that pausing at intervals to remind myself of Him isn't quite what He had in mind for the Christian's climb. He's there all the time. For so long my thinking had been warped: the good principle of starting the day with a "Quiet Time" had become almost legalistic, dividing my day off in sections. It took a fair slice of time to deprogramme me.

St Paul explained this phenomenon in Romans 8 when he said, "Those who live according to the sinful nature have their *minds set* on what that nature desires. The mind of sinful man is death but *the mind controlled by the Spirit* is life and peace." Mindset. At Chefoo I tried to set my mind to follow God in small areas, even when I didn't feel like it, but obedience brought all the joy and feelings I could ever have wanted — afterwards.

Clinging to this slightly higher crag in my thinking, I saw through my new binoculars (which were replacing my blinkers) other little footholds I could clamber towards — anything to get above the misty flats. If I knew I should get up at six am to start the day with God, I was determined to have a mindset that would triumph over feelings that urged, "Why bother? You need the sleep. You've a heavy day ahead." If I needed to prepare a lesson or a talk, I was going to stick at it, even if my tapestry was calling from the craft corner. If someone wanted to thrash things out with me when I'd "had it," I'd try to help whether I felt like it or not. And paramount, if I didn't *like* someone too well, I was going to *act as if I did*. The warm feelings that prompt impulsive giving of oneself weren't there. But — they came eventually.

Fun posters with all sorts of telling phrases began

to pop up worldwide in the seventies. I saw a beauty in our OMF office in Sevenoaks, England. It was blu-tacked to the board room door. A yawning hippo drawled, "After all is said and done, there's not much said and done"! Through the years one that has applied to me is, "Have patience. God isn't finished with me yet." What a volume of patience *God* has had with *me* especially in those early years.

Before we ever left home, John had carefully pointed out to me that when we'd join OMF our salaries would take a deep dive.

"Who cares?" was my response and I thought I meant it. "That doesn't worry me in the least. Money isn't important. I'd rather have no money but have input to God's Kingdom. I'd rather have treasure in heaven."

Hidden in the jungle at Chefoo there was nothing to buy anyway — except perhaps wool. Because the Highlands were cool, holidaymakers loved to knit — something you couldn't do without clammy hands on the plains. I noted joyfully that the ideal wife of Proverbs 31, "selects wool ... and works with eager hands." I made sure, of course, that John knew too that this verse was in the Bible. I let him know that I was sure he'd want me to make this lady my role model.

But on the whole, we staff members were shop-starved! During the Chefoo holidays we would descend on Kuala Lumpur and I with my thoughts anywhere but on "treasure in heaven", would set off on a shopping binge! If we found ourselves there in the Christmas vacation, we would have more pocket money than usual. Friends back in Ireland seldom sent a Christmas parcel. Instead they tucked a little something inside their Christmas cards to replace the fun of present-opening on Christmas morning. And did I ever love to splurge with my Christmas money?

One January we took our holiday in Singapore with our old friend Cecil who had had, in the meantime, the good sense to marry one of our Chefoo teachers (with only the *littlest* help from us). I was so looking forward to getting together with Cecil and Mary.

Two weeks later, back in the Camerons, another breakthrough in my thinking hit me. The simple reflection was that, really, we hadn't seen all that much of Cecil and Mary. And why? I squirmed. I knew why. I'd been out shopping. The Singapore shops were even more attractive than Kuala Lumpur's.

I sat with my Bible in front of me as this exercise of intellect took place. I knew very well whence my thoughts came. That morning God was very firm with me. I could almost hear His Voice. "Okay, you've spent your Christmas money. In fact, you've *over*spent it. How is your husband going to get you through the rest of the quarter? You've barely enough money left to buy stamps for letters home. How long are you going to be like this, Sheila? Totally undisciplined about spending — depending on a Micawber-like philosophy that something will turn up to bail you out. You're putting pressure on John with your wants and whims. And I've spoken to you about this before."

My Bible notes were on Luke 13 where the owner of a fig tree found for a third year no fruit on his tree. "Cut it down," he said, but the gardener replied, "Leave it alone for one more year, and I'll dig around it and fertilize it. If it bears fruit next year, fine! If not, then cut it down."

It seemed as if God was saying to me, "Sheila, I'm giving you one more chance." Selwyn Hughes, who wrote the notes on the story, said that God needs to patiently dig and disturb the barrenness of our lives until the much-sought-for fruit appears. And I realized that my attitude to money needed disturbing, otherwise even God's patience could run out on me.

I greased my mountaineering boots again and haltingly tried to reach the next foothold. I slithered off it. I fell again and again. I caused domestic financial landslides and was left wiping the mud off for weeks. It was this aesthetic eye of mine and the propensity of that eye to select the most expensive item in the shop. The Gardener is still digging round His tree. "Living on less and liking it more" sounds such a very good *principle* ...

Then came a difficult thing to have a mindset on. I discovered God wanted me to sing whether I was blue or not.

This was a shell burst.

At this stage in climbing off the misty flats, my philosophy and prayers ran something like this, "Dear God, I feel in a rotten mood this morning. I hope You don't mind if I don't pray just now. I'll make up for it when the sun shines again. Amen, Sheila."

And I did try to make up for it. I had the temperament of an enthusiastic ant, stunned from time to time by an aerosal can. When everything was going my way a more joyful wife for John could not be found. But *he* knew I didn't live for ever on a high and was totally unimpressed.

Sunday mornings were worst. As teachers at Chefoo School one of our duties was to escort our classes down to the church service in a little old army nissen hut made beautiful by a frontage of stone and a driveway with a lych gate. I loved walking through that lych gate flanked by wooden seats where our

Chefoo choir sat awaiting their entry, robed in white like cherubs.

My own score or so of this little species sat with me during the service and then, like the Grand Old Duke of York, I marched them back again. That was another two miles, mostly uphill. By then, the sun was high in the Camerons' sky. I was hot. I was hungry. I was tired. The morning had been rather too physical for me, taking more from my limited reserves of energy than I could afford — much worse than teaching my children.

By lunch time, it would have been safer to converse with one of the jungle's wild cats than with this Christian missionary who was me. Of course I kept my claws sheathed and no one was supposed to know how bad I felt inside. Invariably, though, John is rather too perceptive; uncomfortably so. He didn't study psychology for nothing and so, I guess, he found Sunday lunch times a bit rough.

That was when I got hold of a book called *Power in Praise* by American army chaplain Merlin Carothers whose first book, *Prison to Praise*, was a best-seller.

The drift of his manuscript was based on verses from the Bible such as, "I will praise the Lord at all times; his praise shall continually be in my mouth!"

In some inexplicable way, the phrase, "at all times" had escaped me before, though I'd been a Christian for years; though I knew the verse — by liver.

A beige dog-eared card had hung over my mother's kitchen sink in Ireland;

> "It's easy enough to be pleasant
> When life goes by like a song,
> But the man worthwhile
> Is the one who can smile

When everything goes dead wrong."
The words had always been with me but until I read
*Power in Praise*, the meaning had eluded me here too.

I reverently handled *Power in Praise* and read all
about Jehoshaphat leading his frightened soldiers into
battle with a choir singing hymns as an hors d'oeuvre.
God explained in 2 Chronicles 20, "Do not be afraid or
discouraged ... For the battle is not yours, but God's."
"You will not have to fight this battle. Take up your
positions; stand firm and see the deliverance the Lord
will give you ..."

That's when Jehoshaphat got his choir together.

"As they began to sing and praise, the Lord set
ambushes against the men ... who were invading
Judah and they were defeated."

*Power in Praise* pointed out to me that the Bible
was full of such patterns. James 1: 2-4: "Dear brothers,
is your life full of difficulties and temptations? Then
be happy, for when the way is rough, your patience
has a chance to grow. So let it grow, and don't try to
squirm out of your problems. For when your patience
is finally in full bloom, then you will be ready for
anything, strong in character, full and complete."

"Count it all joy ... " another translation explained
it. I'd never done that in my whole life. I knew nothing
about it.

So now came this mindset idea again.

"I *will* myself to do it," I told the Lord. "Even if I
don't feel like it ... Even on Sunday mornings."

"John," I called, "do you know what? If you hear
me singing in the shower from now on, it doesn't
necessarily follow that I'm in a good mood."

"Oh," said John, as unfired by my enthusiasms as
ever.

Since then I can recall the notes of hymns sticking

in my constricted throat as I willed myself to sing. I remember when Jonathan went home to boarding school in England, the tears dripping off my chin as I tried to sing Adelaide Proctor's masterpiece,

"I thank Thee more, that all our joy
　　Is touched with pain,
That shadows fall on brightest hours,
　　That thorns remain;
So that earth's bliss may be our guide,
　　And not our chain.


"For Thou, Who knowest, Lord, how soon
　　Our weak heart clings,
Hast given us joys, tender and true,
　　Yet all with wings,
So that we see, gleaming on high,
　　Diviner things."

I remember my Siamese cat leaping off my lap in horror when he discovered I *sang* during my morning Quiet Times. I also remember many dismal failures ...

Just about when the school in the jungle for adults was getting into full swing — I mean, when we were getting into the swing of it — our turn to escort the "Thai party" back to school came up. It was New Year 1972. After Christmas, John, Jonathan and I travelled north to rendezvous with parents all over Thailand before we attempted the marathon journey back.

Jonathan was nine years old and the fun we had showing him Thailand balanced our fear of the hair-raising journeys. One day in Chiang Mai, we found him earnestly engaged in conversation with a Thai man, near the gate of the OMF Guest Home. As John and I hurried down the drive to catch him up, we saw J-boy's head nodding sagely as though taking it in.

"Was your friend speaking English?" I asked a few minutes later.

"Oh no," said Jonathan. "He was telling me all about his travels — in Thai."

"How did that come about?" I managed to ask calmly.

"I just said, 'Bai nai?' and he told me."

*Bai nai* is a Thai greeting which translated is, 'Where are you going?'

But more folks than our extrovert son were talking in Thailand. One subject came up again and yet again. "The Holy Spirit". Even though I was collecting Thai teak, painted umbrellas and all sorts of souvenirs (to take home for others, of course!), I had time to listen.

We took a trip into the hills to tribesland. The missionaries there told us awe-inspiring stories of the power of the Holy Spirit.

We holidayed on a beach in the south. The missionaries there were also discussing this theme. "The Holy Spirit."

"Is this a new emphasis?" I asked John. And I began to understand at last what the word "charismatic" meant in Christian circles. As Michael Griffiths writes in *Serving Grace*, "Notice those wretched inverted commas!"

I found the most lovable and ordinary people were "charismatic". Many of them had the radiancy of Christianity that I was climbing towards. "Can you explain to us more about your thinking on the work of the Holy Spirit?" we asked. I didn't know we were wading into waters where divisions take place. I just wanted the same love for the Lord they had; the same radiancy.

"When we're born again into God's family," said John, "we're born of the Holy Spirit. Having His infilling doesn't need to be a second experience."

I didn't know all the answers but one book I was reading said that when the Holy Spirit renews us, it's like the lid being lifted off the coffee pot and all that's in there already, can flow out.

It seemed to make a lot of sense to me. But people in books who asked God to bless them in this way experienced all sorts of wonderful and joyful things. Many of them found strange words forming in their minds. Then they voiced them and found they were using a new language they'd never learned, to praise God. Mostly, it was described as "speaking in tongues". Some were overwhelmed by the glory of God. Some said they actually felt a feeling go through them in power like an electric shock.

I prayed for this renewal.

Just like the people in books, I prayed. Just like the New Testament Christians in The Acts of the Apostles. But no unusual experience happened. At first I thought God's telex wasn't sending back printouts. And do you know what bailed me out? Mindset.

Listening to a cassette on our return to Chefoo, by David Watson, I heard him say, "How did you accept your salvation from the Lord Jesus? By faith? Even if you didn't feel anything? Right. Accept the gift of the Holy Spirit in the same way."

And I did.

No flashing lights. It was a low-key experience. But I wasn't looking for an experience anyway. I just wanted more of the Lord.

Seventeen years ago John and I joined OMF. Looking back I'm not sure how to put my finger on exactly what changed me in our first term of service at Chefoo. What coloured the grey clay pot radiant? How did I get those wide-angle and zoom lenses?

I can't really pinpoint why I suddenly knew that the Lord Jesus and His Kingdom was the treasure in the field for which a man sold everything he had to possess it.

All I know is my drab Christianity came alive at Chefoo. Sunshine burst through: not through nimbus clouds for the Lord had been real to me in Ireland too, but the sunshine cut a passage through the cumulo-stratus and the Christian sky was blue — bluer than Jonathan's Levis, bluer than anything I'd ever seen before.

Was it because we met as a staff weekly to listen to superb Bible teaching on cassette by David Pawson, then at Millmead Baptist Church? Was it the publication of the Living Bible which I read avidly from cover to cover, that finally dealt a death blow to those blinkers? Was it the "Every Day With Jesus" Bible-reading notes by Selwyn Hughes that Helene, the wife of Ireland's OMF Chairman, started to send? Was it the tiny clamberings of obedience up the slope, off the misty flats? Was it Cynthia's influence? Practising the presence of Christ? Mindset? Renewal by the Holy Spirit?

Whatever it was, it lived. It was real and I was determined to climb on ...

# Reflections

Deep cosmic craters,
shadowed lunar seas,
harsh, dusty, stony, dead
and pock-marked ...

but borrowed light
comes dancing down,
Transforming,
making moonbeams,
shedding silver,
pale but real
I feel
the orb's alight,
ethereal, pearly,
its halo not its own —
just miming moods of day.

Hard human shell
cloud-filled mind and soul,
dry, dust-formed, dreary, dead
and sin-pocked ...

yet Someone's Sun
comes slanting by
Converting,
showering grace-beams,
spilling joy-rays,
poignant, real.
I kneel
and I'm alive,
blood-washed and radiant,
my glory not my own —
just mirroring my Master.

*Sheila Miller*

# 9

# Multishades of local colour

C hefoo's gardener has a smile which spreads warmth like the tropical sunshine. I saw him this year again and wondered right away where his teeth had gone. In the seventies, his teeth had gleamed against a backcloth of peaty features. The dark pigment of his skin was accentuated by work in the sun. Chefoo was "his" school. Dass's initiative, his commitment, his sense of responsibility helped the poinsettias to glow scarlet all year long, pruned the roses, planted the hibiscus, nurtured the citrus trees and shaved back the jungle to give us lawns, a soccer field and an adventure playground.

He was the one who unblocked the dam to aid our water supply. We were proud of our own water — contaminated and brown though it was. Missionary kids love cocoa-coloured baths when the monsoon rains wash more mud into the supply! And Dass was the one who gave the warning about the tiger. "Don't let Jonathan swing on the vines up there," he cautioned one holiday when the school was empty of children, except for our son. "Tiger prints up by the dam. Yes, sir." And it was true. The tiger materialized at the school gate later. It was a Sunday afternoon. The kids were back. Clang! went the school bell. Clang again. "No bike-riding round the drive just now," announced a frenetic voice. We breathed more easily when the tiger disappeared into its own habitat.

But once, some years before the tiger, some years before his keenness to work for us, no contrasts showed in the gardener's face. The unrelieved duskiness revealed his murky thoughts. There was no reason to smile. Daily he gardened — surly, unresponsive and very uninterested in us and our Christianity. Held captive by invisible chains, he fought off any approach that could let him know of freedom in the Lord Jesus Christ.

But one day he was mowing the extensive grass areas around the school with a mighty electric "Flymo". Coping with sloping banks was always a problem but he'd done it before. That day he pushed, then drew the noisy machine towards him. Gradually the tropical growth was surrendering to a clean-shaven, spacious incline.

And then it happened.

The heavy machine lurched too near — too far up the ramp. Its hungry blades glided over Dass's dark foot, protected only by a flimsy canvas shoe.

We found him with a toe almost totally severed.

"The school doctor! And run for the nurse!" Staff and children sped with the message. Dass was carefully carried to Sick Bay. There Dr Lewis spent skill, time and prayer on his unexpected patient. The doctor who had spent years of missionary service in China, had come to our valley in his retirement to care for the health of one hundred children. Compas-

sionately our nurse dressed the injured limb repeatedly and the children prayed for their gardener. They
prayed until he had a healthy new foot.

And Dass never forgot.

That day he'd seen Christian love in practice. In
the weeks that followed he thought about it much.
That's how it was he didn't recoil when Ned next
spoke to him of the love of Christ.

Because of Chefoo, a soul was born. God added
Chefoo's gardener to His church in the Cameron
Highlands. The Tamil Church. Such a church actually
didn't quite exist. The few Indian Christians there met
with the Chinese in a Chinese/English speaking
Gospel Hall. Often we wondered what they understood.

But God's new gardener had Christian impetus
like the apostles in The Acts. Saturday afternoons now
saw him winding his way with a friend to the tea
estates further up the mountain. The tea-pickers were
Hindu, mostly, with no knowledge of the Lord and no
missionary among them.

Saturday by Saturday the two Indian friends
tracted there. A whole year went by and then —
someone believed. Velu, a young man of 24, bread-
winner for a large family because his mother was a
widow.

Velu told his mother about the Lord Jesus. He told
his brothers, his sisters, his friends ...

And then one day, one of those turning-point
days, a knock interrupted John at his desk. Into the
office, in his big soil-caked boots, shady hat in hand,
came Dass with Velu.

"Sir," he began, "Velu's very good. He knows how
to do it. Evangelism, Sir. He wants to go for
training..."

Just at that time a new Bible College had been born right in the south of Malaysia's peninsula. It was very small but it was for Tamil Indians. That's where Velu went with the support of the Chinese Christians and others caring for his mother.

Two years there for a primary-educated tea-estate worker were rough. Isaiah? Turn up Isaiah chapter 26 verse 3. Where was that? Velu wasn't sure that he'd ever heard of Isaiah. He knew only the gospel stories of Jesus. His head wasn't full of knowledge. All he knew was that Jesus had freed him from sin and he wanted his own people to experience this glorious salvation too. Now the teacher was in Ezekiel ... And Joel ... But Velu was still searching for Isaiah. The other students flicked the pages over with seeming lack of difficulty. Velu became totally frustrated. That and the other pressures of his new life in college brought him to the point of despair. And Velu ran away.

He made for Kuala Lumpur, then Penang and eventually — home. The Cameron Highlands. Here Dass who had helped him at the beginning now became his counsellor.

"We need you, Velu. We need you to teach us some day in the tea estates. You can go back. Make notes of what the teacher says. You can look up the references later." Then Dass contacted John again. "Sir, ring the college principal. Couldn't he slow down? He doesn't understand Velu's background..."

Velu returned to college. He completed his course. And now? Now, there's a little Tamil Church in the Cameron Highlands, thirty strong, and through the years the men at Chefoo have cast in their lot to help — Ned, Don, Barry, Jim, Stuart, ...

It's like a once-upon-a-time story with a happy

ending. God adding to His Church and then multi-plying. But Satan is allergic to God's multiplication. *His* forte is division. He has mobilized his demons for attack. Dass needs our prayers. And Velu. And this small Tamil church. The entrenched Hinduism on the tea-estates reacts vigorously against the scattered Christians. And honeymoon days have a habit of coming to an end — even in church life.

Yet, it's gloriously true to say — because of Chefoo, a church was born. Because of Chefoo, by-product blessings have slipped down the mountain slopes from heaven ....

Mrs Lewis, the doctor's wife, Mrs Rowe, a retired OMFer (or meant to be), Shari, Ned's wife, and I greeted the female population of the Camerons with a carefully-worded letter. The letter didn't go to the Malays, of course. The goverment in no way permits proselytizing among Muslims. But we knew Chinese teachers, Indian housewives, expatriate ladies whose husbands managed tea estates, nurses from the Tanah Rata clinic, plus this contact and that scattered here and there over the plateau.

"Would you like," the letter asked, "to come to a Bible-study group together? RSVP," and we four signed the invitation.

Response was so positive that we felt quite overwhelmed with delight. Even Lorraine wanted to come.

Lorraine is a New Zealander. An extremely elegant New Zealander. Lorraine was so sophisticated that I found difficulty saying the right things if I ever got talking to her. Lorraine attended the services at the army nissen-hut church but I thought she wouldn't ever want to know a missionary, let alone study the Bible with a group of our type.

But the Bible studies started and Lorraine was always there; bright, vivacious and very much at home in her Camerons' community. Each fortnight we met in a different house. Lorraine, married to a Chinese architect, was the perfect hostess. At her home, I stood in the wings, in awe.

Saturdays were days I really liked at Chefoo. I liked most days (except Sunday mornings) as I was in love with my job. But *Saturdays*! No pressure. No timetable. The day to myself to do my own thing. Someone else to answer the school phone. Saturdays, specially the mornings, because, remember, I'm a lark, were great. Cynthia once said to me, "Sheila, you're a real rooster!" Lark sounds just that bit more graceful!

Early one Saturday morning, when John was still sleeping off his week of late nights, my Bible reading was in Romans. As I read the first chapters about the hopelessness of people without God and supplemented my study by listening to David Pawson's thoughts about it all on cassette, I got to thinking, *Well, Sheila, what are you doing for lost humanity? God seems to be taking the brakes off us all. The world is slithering downhill into hell.*

Then I thought to myself, *How would you do anything about it, if you were going to*?

I did a double-take. I've never considered myself an evangelist. But the sunny alcove where these reflections took place seemed alive with the presence of God. Was the Holy Spirit indicating something to me?

*Dear God,* I wondered, *do You mean I need to be ready for a "happening" with You?*

The room was silent.

The impression of the Lord's presence persisted.

Well, what would I do? What could I say? Who

would I say it to? Along what lines was I to say something?

The early morning quiet still encircled me.

*I'd better get ready,* I decided. *Perhaps I've got to help someone today. Perhaps I might even need to lead someone to the Lord Jesus. Do I know how to do that?*

I tried to work out how to start a conversation from scratch. I bathed in God's presence like at home in winter I would snuggle into our electric blanket. I looked here and there in the Scriptures for what might be helpful verses. Psalm 37 was good, I thought. Maybe that was because I love that poem myself. At our goodbye services in Ireland I had quoted verse 4 repeatedly, "Delight yourself in the Lord and he will give you the desires of your heart." That's what had happened to me in coming to Chefoo.

I made some notes, prayed some prayers, plugged the phone in again and waited. Waited for my caller.

All day long I waited. Nobody came.

"I was so *sure*," I wailed to John at bedtime. "I don't think I could be mistaken that the inner voice I heard was God's."

"I don't think you're mistaken either, Sheila," said John, "but perhaps you've got your timing wrong."

Sundays follow Saturdays and then came that absorbing school week which was my lot. I forgot all about Saturday morning's little incident. Perhaps yet again, my imagination had run away with me ...

Linda's home, a few weeks later, was the venue for our next Bible study. Linda was a new Indian bride. John and I had been thrilled to be guests at her wedding. Unexpectedly John had been called on to "say grace" before the meal. The mix of Hindus, Muslims, Buddhists and the few Christians were as taken aback as we were. Their response to John's prayer was choice — spontaneous applause!

The clapping died down and we made a great effort to be part of the group. "Do you work here in the Camerons?" John asked the Malaysian opposite him.

The man fixed his dark eyes on John. Fixed them with a hypnotic-type stare which quite articulately said, "I've heard your question. I'll answer it in a moment. Can't just yet. I've something in my mouth right now."

John's blue eyes stared back and waited. He couldn't look away. The friendly national was enjoying the local delicacy of chickens' feet. You slip the claws into your mouth and suck: suck until every vestige of flavour has been relished. Then before John's astonished gaze, he raised his hand to deliver the bones. One spit — out came the remains of a chicken's claw. Two — another followed. Three. I hope John didn't look as mesmerized as he felt. But the man's stare held him until seven bones were ejected. Only after that could conversation continue.

Linda was now living in the Malay *kampung* in a house on stilts. I'd never been to a Bible study in this kind of local house before.

Somehow I was the penultimate girl to grope for my shoes on her porch afterwards. The Chefoo van was waiting at the bottom of the wooden steps.

A hand touched my shoulder. Lorraine's. Lorraine was last in our shoe-claiming line. "Sheila," she whispered, "I've got to talk to you."

I looked up from my buckles. Her eyes were full of tears.

Wouldn't it seem like a delightful coda after a symphonic movement by God to invite Lorraine to have tea with me? I did that. Yet I had absolute palpitations about it. I didn't know what to give her to eat.

But Lorraine didn't seem to notice that the pancakes were like leather. She and her family were huddled under an umbrella of despair. As she unfolded her story, the gravity of the situation struck me like something from a TV horror film. I could barely grasp that what she said could be happening in the modern-day, civilized, cool Camerons.

Menacing letters. Extortion demands, wholesale harassment, *or else* ... The "or else" in all its malevolence threatened violence, kidnap, and even death for the entire family.

"Every time our dogs bark, we wonder if someone is prowling; lurking round our house. When we go out, we don't know if we'll get back safely. I can't take it. Not any more. There've been four letters now. Does it mean we've got to get out of the Camerons?" And she burst into tears.

Outside, in a different world, the Chefoo children played in high spirits. Outside, in the jungle trees, the cicadas whirred in the afternoon sunshine. Inside, Lorraine and I sat shrouded in oppression.

"Lorraine," I faltered, searching for words to express my empathy, "have you ever read King David's poem in Psalm 37?"

"What is it?"

"'Do not fret'," I started, "'because of evil men ...'"

"Does it really say that in the Bible?" asked this girl with the green luminous eyes.

"Yes. It says they are like grass that will soon wither."

"What else does David say?"

"'Trust in the Lord and do good';" I read "'dwell in the land and enjoy safe pasture. Delight yourself in the Lord and he will give you the desires of your heart. Commit your way to the Lord; trust in him and he will do this: He will make your righteousness shine like the dawn, the justice of your cause like the noonday sun. Be still before the Lord and wait patiently for him; do not fret when men succeed in their ways, when they carry out their wicked schemes. Refrain from anger and turn from wrath; do not fret ... '"

"God doesn't want you to be upset," I explained. "The position you're in is of crisis proportion but God's promises can stand up to our crises. Do you know what He said in Romans?"

"Tell me."

"'And we know that in all things God works for the good of those who love him'."

"Could you mark that place for me?" asked Lorraine. "'... in all things', even in this nightmare."

No magic wand broke through the clouds, waving goodbye to Lorraine's circumstances. She had to live through them. But God poured in all His love, His reassurances and His comfort. It took time before this new friend of mine could say, "It was dreadful but through it all, I found God in a new way."

I started popping over to visit, to lend a book, to chat, to pray. *I* was the one who came away blessed. The stories she told of her adventures in faith thrilled me: they opened another window which wafted in the fresh new things God can do.

The Cameron Highlands still beckon the Miller Trio at holiday time. And Lorraine is always there, mature and attractive in her love for her Lord. We still talk of our adventures in faith; we chitchat about this and that and have a go at setting the world to rights during our coffee mornings. But she doesn't serve leather pancakes.

# Dial-a-prayer

*On and off all day I've tried.*
*I can't get any answer.*

*Was I calling*
*a wrong number?*
*Is he out?*
*I'll try once more —*
*check in the big book —*
*dial, carefully.*
*A busy signal! Could*
*God have left his receiver*
*off the hook?*
*(Someone's at the door.*
*They'll have to wait.)*
*Dial "O".*
*"Operator — is this number*
*still in service? Yes?"*
*Spin it again. And still*
*no answer. I'm*
*positive my line's not*
*out of order. (Will*
*that knocking never stop?)*

*His phone rings on.*
*Easy for him to say "Need help?*
*Call on me any time!"*
*What if I can't get through?*
*What if he's gone?*

*or could that knocking be*
*him*
*calling on*
*me?*

© *Luci Shaw*

# 10

## A fifty gram ball of random-coloured wool

Flopping days and holidays between school terms were even better than Saturday mornings. Term time was what made Chefoo tick but the pressure was on full blast — teaching, taking my turn to lead the new ladies' Bible studies, library duties, constant entertaining, scribbling stories and mothering — if Jonathan decided to be around. The call of the great outdoors with 99 friends was more in his line.

Mostly, we Chefoo staff, when vacation was due, liked to grace the yellow tropical beaches of the peninsula, wallow in the warm water of the Indian Ocean and try to get as brown as the nationals — something they could never fathom. Once I looked along the row of jars in our local grocery-cum-chemist's shop and asked for suntan cream. Delighted with himself, the assistant produced a tube labelled "Skin Whitener"!

Despite the lure of the seaside, I said to John one year, "How about having our holidays right up here where the air is cool and we'll just relax in the OMF holiday bungalow for two weeks?" The Bungalow was wellknown territory to us. It lay one mile away along the twisty road from the school.

"You *sure*?" asked the others in puzzled concern. "Stay in the Camerons? A mile away?"

We were sure, and we even packed case-loads of stuff to prove it.

John was a member of the local golf club. The setting for the golfers was almost out of this world. Nowhere, John thought, was there such a challenge to par or birdie. Nowhere could there be such scenery. The fresh fun of the game or the waiter from the Merlin Hotel bringing a far-flung ball out to the course on a silver tray, far outweighed the time John disturbed a hornet's nest searching for one of those elusive balls in the rough.

My goal for the holiday was different. (I am not athletic.) A new craze had hit us females — west *and* east. CROCHET. My aim for that fortnight was to master the craft of creating doubles, trebles and shells.

The holiday bungalow sat on its own little plateau surrounded by garden, like some fairy-tale castle of yesteryear. The tower had windows on every wall. Two pictures which were really masks, concealed peepholes. You could see right out on either side of the tower, down into the valleys. That bedroom had once been a gambling den. Mahjong. And spies had kept a secret eye open for the police.

Now peepholes and windows surveyed a green lawn, flower beds, an "existing tree", its knobbly roots elbowing out of the green where the swing was tied, a barbecue corner, a badminton court ... They peeked at us — the holidaying missionaries, lolling on deck chairs, reading, bird watching, having a game or — crocheting.

I was hooked. I dreamed of crocheted shells. Last

thing at night I thought of it and decided what a shame it is that mortals have to waste so much time recharging their batteries in sleep. First thing in the morning there were my squares fairly yelling at me to hurry up and get started again — at once, even if it were only six am.

My Bible lay closed on our bedroom desk.

Aeons had drifted by since I'd learned to start each day with a Bible reading. But a ball of wool, a fashionable pattern and a crochet hook were driving a wedge between me and the Lord. Aeons ago, too, I'd studied developmental psychology at college. The first lectures just about bowled me over. I caught a valuable insight on how to handle, not only the children I'd teach, but myself. Freud gave me skeleton keys to areas I didn't have access to before. When I was falling apart, I could trace back causes and try to get myself together again.

When I caught sight of my closed Bible, I could see, therefore, that I had a problem. Festinger's Theory of Cognitive Dissonance! I also knew, though, that recognition of the problem was the first step towards solving it.

One of my little aids to help me take right decisions is to project myself (plus all the enthusiastic feelings that God has mixed in His recipe of me) a few weeks' hence. "Would you prefer," I asked my psyche, "at the end of your holiday, a beautiful new crocheted jacket OR one in-the-making plus your hours of fellowship with God?"

Of late the Lord had been so precious to me that I was in no doubt. At the end of the holiday, I would have wished I had spent more time with Him.

Mindset.

After this little session of self-analysis, I made up

my mind to stay in our room until coffee break every day. I would sit at my desk and study the Psalms — I mean some of them.

"You'll miss the garden at its best," Satan told me, "You know how fickle the Camerons' weather is ..."

But I wanted no more misty flats' experiences. Instead I had peace.

Psalm 16 became a favourite. I loved the fresh new Living Bible translation. I learned the words:

"The Lord Himself is my inheritance, my prize
... my *highest* joy! ...
He sees that I am given pleasant brooks and
meadows as my share! ...
I will bless the Lord who counsels me; he
gives me wisdom in the night,
He tells me what to do ...
You have let me experience the joys of life and
the exquisite pleasures of your own
eternal presence"

The little Chinese cleaning girl brushed round my feet as I saw that "those choosing other gods shall all be filled with sorrow". And I knew that even crochet could be an idol.

Never did the three of us have a happier holiday. Chefoo's gates welcomed back a glowing trio — refreshed physically and spiritually. Lots of golf balls lost and found, miles of bike-riding behind J-boy and netfuls of glorious butterflies. Plus a fair amount of crochet accomplished!

I hadn't reckoned on the Lord's rich reimbursements, though. As a direct result of my holiday hobby, the Poncho Club was born. Actually it didn't quite intend to be a Poncho Club. It was to be "Yarn Along" but when I spread all my crochet patterns over the wooden floor to inspire the senior girls, I found they didn't even take under their notice the ties for father at

Christmas, the stuffed animals grinning back at them, the dolls' clothes, the pencil cases, tea-cosies ... No, nothing like that. Everyone wanted to crochet a poncho.

My mother had sent us a huge box of wool from Ireland. Just spilling it out all over the place was inspiration itself. Paddypaws, Jonathan's cat, loved it! Cliff Richard, for years Britain's top pop singer and a Christian, went on the record player and off we'd go — two hours at the weekends of fun, rapport and creativity.

And then an unusual corollary added itself. The domestic staff, a dozen or so Chinese village girls, caught the bug. Crochet had hit the craft headlines in a big way, just as patchwork does right now. Would I teach them too?

Few of them had much idea of English and I had no Chinese but round a long table in a classroom, demonstration was enough. I stuck in a "yes" here and a "no" there and someone translated a pattern if necessary.

The important thing to me wasn't that these girls learned to crochet. It was the relationship that built up between us because of the fun we were having. Most of them were Buddhist. But, one day, the few Christians asked if I'd take a weekly Bible study with them. They'd bring their friends, they said.

I wasn't good at it. I wasn't clued-in enough to Chinese culture. I needed an interpreter. But for a while I tried.

All this because God blessed a holiday decision. When I let go my pitiful little struggle with wool, the Lord totally turned the tables. He is a *great* Lord.

Way back in London, when John and I had attended OMF's Candidate School, I remember asking some knowledgeable missionary if I'd have "neighbours" in the Cameron Highlands. *Heatherlea* had been planted right bang in the middle of all sorts — neighbours who came to our parties, to Bible studies, who were invited to the meetings we used to attend, to whom I loaned books ... I liked neighbours. I wanted to go on having them even if the Camerons were sparsely populated. And God found me those neighbours — friends from various races.

And although we staff members weren't out there like *real* missionaries in the front line, we had a wonderful back-up work going on ... all because of Chefoo.

# In No Strange Land

*O world invisible, we view thee,*
*O world intangible, we touch thee,*
*O world unknowable, we know thee,*
*Inapprehensible, we clutch thee!*

*Does the fish soar to find the ocean,*
*The eagle plunge to find the air —*
*That we ask of the stars in motion*
*If they have rumour of thee there?*

*Not where the wheeling systems darken,*
*And our benumbed conceiving soars! —*
*The drift of pinions, would we hearken,*
*Beats at our own clay-shuttered doors.*

*The angels keep their ancient places; —*
*Turn but a stone, and start a wing!*
*'Tis ye, 'tis your estranged faces,*
*That miss the many-splendoured thing.*

*But, when so sad thou canst not sadder,*
*Cry — and upon thy so sore loss*
*Shall shine the traffic of Jacob's ladder*
*Pitched betwixt Heaven and Charing Cross.*

*Yea, in the night, my Soul, my daughter,*
*Cry — clinging Heaven by the hems ...*
*And so, Christ walking on the water*
*Not of Gennesareth, but Thames!*

*Francis Thomson*

# 11

## Shocking Pink

Jonathan's crutches clopped softly as we hustled him into Kuala Lumpur's airport. A Malaysian jumbo jet was soon to swallow the three of us. In sixteen hours' time we'd be home.

It was good to sink into the allotted cushions. High with excitement, despite concern for J-boy, I could hardly wait to see our folk again. It was four and a quarter years since we'd landed on tropical soil. My mother had requested our choice of menu for the welcome home meal in Ireland. John ordered plum-pudding (although it was June), I settled for one of her delicious lemon meringue pies and Jonathan wanted to taste *real* milk. He'd put in a bid for, "A pint, please, Grandma — in a bottle."

But this loading up to cross the world was a baneful business. And it was all happening differently from our original plans. Were we upside-down in our thinking? Or had the Lord turned us the right way up? We'd packed for a year's home assignment only. All our household things were still at Chefoo — even though our suggested stint of missionary service was over.

An airline steward strode down the aisle calling for Mrs Miller. He deposited an exotic bouquet of orchids in my lap. From Richard and Helen — OMF friends in Malaysia. We'd taught their boys *and* we were going home to live in *their* house. England, not Ireland. *Hey There*, not *Heatherlea*.

At first John and I had been highly enthusiastic about berthing at Chefoo again and becoming full-time members of OMF. But as the time drew near to take the decision a cold fear like an elastic band threatened to choke me. The plan to return to the school in the jungle, which we longed to do, went hand-in-hand with committing Jonathan to boarding school at home for his secondary education, which we did *not* long to do.

Other missionaries' kids had left Chefoo for school in their homelands. That's how it was done. Should we do the same? We could only guess at the trauma it would involve.

Whenever the trees weren't calling to be climbed, whenever the trails didn't have to be hiked, the superb butterflies to be caught and set, his banana-saddled bike to be ridden, we'd try to elicit J-boy's feelings about boarding school for *him*.

Jonathan's thoughts on the subject were flagrantly positive. We felt rather taken aback! From his point of view nothing could be worse than having a school where your father was the headmaster and your mother had taught you for one interminable year. It would be "real cool" to be like other kids with your parents nowhere on the horizon!

So Jonathan's name was put on the waiting list for Monkton Combe School, Bath, in England's West Country. And we indicated to OMF that if there was a place for us, we'd like to return.

It just couldn't be, of course, that we'd live our year's home leave in *Heatherlea*. Not with the Irish Sea between Jonathan and us. That was when Richard and Helen offered us their beautiful house in Weston-super-Mare. But first, we'd hop over to Ireland to see everyone again.

"So Jonathan's going to boarding school?" said this one and that.

"Yes. Monkton Combe School in Bath. It's a Christian school; one our mission uses; near to the big rambling hostel, Donnington Hurst, where J-boy can go at half-terms and holidays. That's why we're going to live over there for the year. Weston-super-Mare is only an hour's drive from Bath."

"How can you let him go to boarding school limping like that?" asked Pat. Pat was the friend whose timetable worked alongside mine — the "kindred spirit" with whom I grew up, having found each other in Portstewart where she too had been evacuated during the war years.

"What's wrong with Jonathan's leg?" asked another. This "other" received our news circulars in which every detail of J-boy's problem had been spelled out. It's one of the isolated dashes of cold water missionaries are prone to receive when they discover some interested folk aren't so interested after all!

Speaking at Missionary Conferences was a big feature of home assignment. One verse from the Bible cropped up in our messages frequently. The Lord Jesus had said, "Let me assure you that no one has given up anything — home, brothers, sisters, mother, father, children or property — for love of me and to tell others the Good News, who won't be given back a hundred times over, homes, brothers, sisters, mothers, children and lands — with persecutions. All these will be his here on earth and in the world to come he shall have eternal life."

Back in England, we found Richard and Helen's house near the seaside, one of God's "hundredfolds".

"Look Mum," Jonathan called as he hobbled from room to room, "See this? The archway's padded. It's velvet! And look at this, you just twist this little knob and you can have your lights high" he demonstrated, "or you can have them dimmed. And have you noticed over here ...?"

This house was a dream — in a village lane; Wisteria Avenue. Enormous kitchen windows looked out on cows in the farm next door — the cows that made the back-up group for Jonathan's trombone playing.

"Give me Middle C," J-boy would shout from the open kitchen door and then blast their pitch for them.

Those cows echoed Middle C and any other note Jonathan chose to demand of them until our kitchen rocked with laughter.

All furlough long *Hey There* called its name to our friends and family because one of its boasts was five bedrooms, *Yes, I could really enjoy life here,* I thought, *if only Jonathan's ankle was better.*

The fact was that a few years previously Jonathan had torn a ligament in his foot. That poor foot had been treated with hot wax baths, with inspection by Kuala Lumpur's best consultant, with a plaster cast to the knee for weeks, with anything anyone could think of, but as soon as it began to mend and Jonathan was let loose on the playing field again, the ligament played up. It ruined many a game for him and prevented him from trying to win the 100 yard sprint on his final Sports' Day. To a primary school child the torn ligament was one gross calamity.

John and I were concerned, too, about subjecting Jonathan to boarding school with this injury.

"Supposing he can't play the games that his body is built for ... " I said to John. "Suppose his ankle makes school life a misery ... "

"Life at Monkton Combe won't be a misery. He can't wait to get there," stated the phlegmatic John. "However, I do think we should see a specialist again."

But Jonathan remained with his clipped wings and his supportive bandage.

One evening in August when we'd been home two months, John was to speak at the little flood-lit holiday church on the hill in Weston-super-Mare. Our *Heatherlea* neighbours were with us having a vacation and John had us all roped into the programme. My part was to review, "Power in Praise"!

That afternoon John disappeared from *Hey There's* sitting room to be alone with God and His message. The Bible passage for the service was Mark Chapter 2 about the four men who found their way to Jesus with a paralyzed friend on his bed. The only way in was to dig a hole in the roof. "The Man with Ten Legs", the sermon was called!

That summer evening with us all taking part was quite perfect. Back home in *Hey There*, Florence and I sent our kids upstairs to get ready for bed.

I was standing in the all-mod-con kitchen buttering biscuits for a bedtime snack. The cows were shrouded in the evening dusk.

Thud! Thump! The silence was suddenly shattered. A tornado in the form of Jonathan came clumping down the stairs and burst in through the kitchen door.

Just like a tornado would, he swept my feet from under me.

"Mum!" he yelled. "Look!"

Butter poised on the knife, I reeled round. Jonathan was waving his supportive bandage high like a flag.

"Mum!" he exclaimed, his cheeks red, brown curls tousled. He looked like a Muscovite in a fur hat.

My response wasn't exactly cerebral. I stared at him, scared to death because the heavy crepe was fluttering around in the air. Worse, he had his two feet firmly on the ground without it. From this alcove and that of *Hey There*, the rest of the household was gathering in the dusky kitchen to see what the detonation was all about.

Jonathan jumped on the floor — up and down, over and over again. Even the cows could have felt the earth tremor.

"Jonathan!" Now I was really scared. "Your foot, pet. You'll damage that ligament again!"

"But the ache's gone!" Jonathan was insisting. Taking off his bandage each night had been a painful experience. But tonight was different. The released ankle hadn't objected. Jonathan jumped again to prove his point.

How is it that when life calls for some great manifesto, we miss it? I, with my wildly enthusiastic temperament, lamely said, "Better go and have your bath now." It was because I didn't really believe what he was saying. And because I was worried.

The children climbed the stairs again noisily, and we adults were left with our biscuits.

John quietly spoke. "Did J-boy say his foot was better?"

"Yes," I said, quite put out about it all. "He'll have done a lot of damage acting around like that ..."

"Sheila, I want to tell you something," said John.

"This afternoon, as I thought of the faith the four men displayed in carrying their friend to Jesus, I wondered if I could dig a hole in the roof of *our* difficulty and bring Jonathan to Jesus too.

"It's like Pat said. How *can* we send him to boarding school as he is — not able to play the games that are a schoolboy's life? This afternoon, I carried him — ligament, bandages, crutches and all to Jesus."

The biscuits lay on the bread-board untouched.

"We've prayed before... " I began, rather doubtfully.

"This was different," explained John. "It was as if the Lord was telling me that preaching on a healing miracle when I myself had a lame son, wasn't on. I didn't tell you about my prayer of faith. I didn't tell anyone. I just waited to see what would happen."

Jonathan went off to Monkton Combe with a healthy foot. He played rugby, ran cross-country, joined the rowing club, did pot-holing in the Mendip Hills and boisterously got into anything physical that was going.

Through the years there have been occasional sprains in *both* ankles, gore tracks from rugger boots along his back, there have been a split shin and cracks on the head. But all through his secondary and tertiary education, he's played his way on this team and that, with two working ankles.

South West England's halcyon summer days were coming to an end. D-Day was looming up — the day in September when we'd deliver J-boy to Monkton Combe School.

"It's time we got his uniform together," I said to John, "because I'll need to make sure I have enough days left to get everything name-taped."

OMF had given us a cheque towards buying his

new clothes. We knew it wouldn't cover everything but we decided to make a start.

The outfitter's shop was in Bristol. Ambitiously the three of us climbed into the old Avenger we'd bought to press forward with making the purchases.

"Have you got the list?" asked John.

"Yes. It's — er, rather long."

"Well, let's investigate anyway," John suggested.

The school outfitter's had a little bell on the door signifying that a customer had arrived. A sombre-suited salesman greeted us with a bow. He looked as though he'd spent his life being obsequious to wealthy parents. That was when I felt the butterflies starting to flutter somewhere inside.

Intuition kept me from handing him our list.

"What would madam like to see first?" asked the suave Englishman.

My Irish accent was choking me but I managed, "Can we look at the winter coats?" After all, if we bought nothing else, J-boy had to be warm.

I knew it. The navy duffle coat cost more than all the money we had in hand.

In absolute consternation we checked the price of the school suit, the grey trousers, the Monkton Combe blazer with its white crest on the pocket. I groaned. Would Jonathan *ever* own one?

Monkton Combe School is one of England's public schools. Normally John and I could never have afforded to send Jonathan there, but at that time the government gave a substantial grant towards the fees to voluntary workers abroad. They did not give a grant towards the uniform!

"Well, we'll just settle for this and that today," I said and bought three pairs of big woolly knee socks.

"Mum," challenged Jonathan as we reboarded the

Avenger, "I thought we were coming to Bristol to buy my school uniform!"

"Yes. I think we may have to make another trip," I said, hoping it sounded plausible.

"But, Mum, is there time? I've to go to school in a couple of weeks!"

"I know." I tried to speak calmly but inside I felt black with despair. My mood resembled a tropical sky before a thunderstorm. What were we going to do?"

The atmosphere in the car was pretty grim. Somewhere along the road I stumbled out with, "Let's all sing together!" But I wondered if "Power in Praise" would really work this time.

I thought of other money OMF had given to help fit us out for a winter at home. Gone. Marks and Spencer had made sure of that with its rows of pyjamas that John badly needed, the summer dresses I couldn't buy in Malaysia, shirts, negligee ... Marks and Sparks had everything you could ever possibly want. And we couldn't take them back to the shop: we were enjoying wearing it all already.

Two months of British shops in 1974's summer was making me neurotic, I decided. It was as if John and I had done a Rumpelstiltskin. Four years had changed life at home so vastly. Inflation had hit the country. The coinage had gone decimal. We were totally at sea. It seemed to me that the new penny wasn't of any more value than the old. And there used to be 240 of them in a pound sterling. I couldn't believe the price of the groceries. I spent precious energy diving from this shop to that looking for a bottle of orange juice one penny cheaper. And when I got to the checkout girl, she didn't exactly welcome me as I fumbled with the unfamiliar coins, feeling quite sure a florin should be worth 20 pence and not 10.

Before we left for Asia, we'd been warned about the culture shock we would experience in a new land. It was *nothing*; nothing compared with returning to Britain and trying to pick up the strands of living. In fact, the only memory of "culture shock" registering with me in 1970 was sandwiched between sentences during an interview with our Course Supervisor. She was American. Above her office desk, my astonished gaze hit a Map of the World pinned on the wall. The Americas, the entire long north to south of them, were bang on centre from one Pole to the other.

Where were the bright red British Isles? I'd never seen a "foreign" Map of the World before. It took a little time for me to realize that the United Kingdom was not the focus of attention for other nationalities. "Britannia rule the waves" and all that didn't even enter their thinking! And, to exacerbate my discontentment, I discovered that Singapore's new airport Time Map has the Far East as *its* axis. The British Isles is just about on there and no more — falling off the far end.

But arriving in them after our years away, we experienced a severe dose of culture shock in reverse.

I thought of the red blouse I'd wanted so badly in Malaysia and couldn't find anywhere. At home I trundled out happily to make this long-awaited purchase. Row upon row, hanger upon hanger, line upon line of blouses. Quite incapable of making the choice, I fought my way out of the shop, shaking — one of the rare occasions I've let Marks and Spencer down!

Yes, I decided, shopping had become a nightmare. And now there was this uniform to buy. We were determined to keep the worry of expenses from Jonathan and from everyone except our heavenly Father.

"We just need to pray," I told John. "That's what people in books do. You tell the Lord your need and a fat cheque arrives in the post. I've read about it time and again."

"Listen, Sheila," said John, "this is a totally different situation from what you've read in your God-will-provide books. This is a problem of our own making. We've overspent. Too many things too soon. We can't expect the Lord to bail us out because we've mismanaged our accounts."

*Hey There's* hall carpet began to wear thin as I ran to search our letter box several times a day in the hope, all the same, that God would help us. No cheques. No anonymous donors. No envelopes slipped under the door. Nothing.

"We've been slow learners in this area," John pointed out. "Perhaps God needs to teach us a few lessons." Nevertheless we prayed fervently. Last thing at night, we prayed. First thing in the morning. At intervals all day long. "Dear God, what are we going to do? We have nobody but You to help us. Lord, imagine what it would do to a new boy to go to school for the first time with no uniform! Please send us the money we need. Appreciatively in advance, John and Sheila."

The days slipped by, in bicycle-riding jaunts around new haunts for Jonathan, a flurry of worry for me about the missing clothes I was supposed to sew name tapes on, and queries in John's mind as to why three different people who owed us money didn't think to repay it. John thought that God could time that money to come.

But still we searched the letter-box and the door mat in vain.

"If *I* were taking the consequences, I could accept it," I wailed to John, "but because of us, this is happening to Jonathan. It'll do dreadful things to him if he's different from every other boy."

There were no pat answers and no further visits to the Bristol outfitter.

Instead we packed Jonathan's things (minus the big bulk of them) in his trunk and headed off on the first day of term with a very puzzled eleven-year old. We had concluded we'd just have to take him shopping in a few weeks' time when our new quarter's remittance arrived.

The English countryside was at its beautiful best to herald the approach of autumn. The once-white Avenger nosed its way through quaint villages towards our hour of doom. The handiwork of the Creator was overshadowed by our circumstances. Other people, even Hudson Taylor himself, the great founder of our mission, had his needs met. Had our heavenly Father let us down?

Parking in the immaculate grounds was an ordeal. Elegant mothers, wealthy fathers and uniformed schoolboys spilled out of automobiles with this year's registration plates. It reminded me of Tennyson's "The Charge of the Light Brigade":

> "Cannons to right of us
> Cannons to left of us
> Cannons before us
> Volleyed and thundered ... "

The thunder deafened our joy in what should have been a momentous occasion.

The herd instinct in us followed a group towards one of the buildings. Some were carrying great armfuls of boys' clothing. I thought I heard a phrase being bandied around. Could I have got it right?

"John," I whispered, "I think there's a secondhand shop in here."

Yes! Mothers were unloading grey and navy outfits ad infinitum. Their sons had grown taller. Could anyone else use them? Well — *could* they!

I hope we approached the coat-hangers at a circumspect pace. I hope we did. But in fact I know I acted like a guided missile. I felt like an enchanted child following a Pied Piper. His music drew my eyes to one of those beautiful, warm, winter, school-regulation duffle coats!

"I wonder would that fit our son?" I said to the girl in charge. "Oh," she replied, "there's a label pinned to this one. That means it's probably sold already."

The Pied Piper music began to fade within me.

"Wait!" the young assistant matron called. "The note says, 'TO BE RESERVED FOR AN OMF CHILD, PLEASE'".

It was hard not to weep — with joy. Our Lord had known all the time. We emerged from that room with the lot — right down to rugby gear. "You don't need to pay for these items now," the girl explained. "We'll put them on your account." At Christmas we knew we'd have the money to meet it.

Our new schoolboy started Monkton Combe with everything he needed.

It wasn't a sad farewell. *Hey There* was only an hour's journey away ....

# Donegal

*Here on the dim horizon the humped hills,*
*Blurred with rain, turn their backs to the wind*
*And huddle together. The fretted grey Atlantic*
*Boils at their feet. And then the cloud is gone*
*And silver light spills from the sky again.*

*This is my magic ground. Oh may no bitter fate*
*Prevent my returning,*
*And let there be this light on the water for me*
*At the end of all journeys.*

Evangeline Paterson

# 12

# *Autumn's Twilight*

John drew the borrowed red mini into a lay-by — a picture-postcard spot. County Antrim's "White Rocks" towered above us: the North Atlantic breakers foaming round "The Wishing Arch" spit their spray on our windscreen: Northern Ireland's sky hung grey and loweringly — its favourite colour. But its scowl couldn't dampen our inward glow. Portrush was just around the corner and we were en route to the main missionary conference of the year there.

We had our act together. Our aim was to tell any part of the world that would listen, about Chefoo. True to our teaching professional hearts, we had a visual aid to assist us. It was a bicycle wheel. The hub represented Chefoo. Around the perimeter were Southeast Asia's countries where OMF's missionaries were free to preach the Good News of the gospel because their children were safely cared for at Chefoo.

The wheel with its psychedelic labels lay waiting in the boot. "Do you think," asked John, "we're really going to get this message across?"

"Well, we're certainly intense about it!"

"Should we introduce just a little more levity?"

I groaned. That was sure to mean something like an act up front, which John, born to drama, excelled in and which made me want to merge with the decor.

"*I* know!" John's normally phlegmatic voice held a ring of excitement. He'd had one of his ideas. His ideas were usually vastly different from mine. "We'll sing a song," he said, "an Irish song with our own Chefoo words!"

As the White Rocks looked on, the two of us sat and composed a jingle with prolific apologies to the writer of the lyric, *The Mountains of Mourne*.

This OMF Mission's a wonderful sight
With the missionaries working by day and by night,
    They don't look for money or treasures on earth
    But there's gangs helping folk from the East to new birth.
At least, when we joined them that's what we were told
So we just took a hand digging heavenly gold!
    And now after four years, we're happy to tell
    That this mission's for us and we want to work well.
There were mishes in Thailand, Laos and Vietnam,
The Philippine Islands, Singapore and Taiwan,
    Cambodia claimed some and also Japan
    To Hong Kong, Indonesia, Korea, they ran.
Not to mention Malaysia — the nicest of all
The missionaries flew obeying God's call
    Soon nationals believed — it all was worthwhile,
    When a problem loomed large, cramping missionary style.
Some missionaries married and had children, so
Another five years meant to school they must go.
    They looked round about them; the problem was this

Those schools taught in languages they couldn't
lisp.
OMF had a brainwave; it came from the Lord,
To teach all the children — it seemed such a horde,
To help all the parents, what else could they do?
The obvious thing was to have a Chefoo!
The school's in the mountains, five thousand feet
high,
The land is Malaysia so jungle is nigh.
But deep in that jungle a valley was found
Just right for white children to scamper around.
Green acres, a stream, trees to climb — what a place!
Enough to bring smiles to each little kid's face!
So there they built classrooms and dormitories,
too.
The name of the school? You remember?
CHEFOO!
The staffing's a problem — the school's far away
With one hundred children to care for each day.
We heard of the vacancies, thought we'd apply
And OMF said they would give us a try.
Now after four years we want to go back
The school tugs our hearts though the children aren't
black.
I teach the ten-year olds: John's the headmaster,
The days couldn't possibly fly any faster.
We scrub them and feed them and put them to bed,
We teach them and cram needful facts in each head.
Two thousand nails must be cut every week,
We're sure the dorm aunties must often feel weak!
But in faraway places the gospel is told
While we care for the five-to-eleven-year-old.
So, if folk trust in Jesus, as we pray they will do
It's partly because there's a school called Chefoo!
This assignment which OMF called "deputation
work" was quite good fun, we decided — even though

an elderly lady caught my hand after one meeting and asked, "Sheila, do you ever see Prudence out in those parts?" My friend Prudence was a missionary in Uganda.

One evening a prayer meeting was scheduled for us in County Donegal. Londonderry, our base for that month, is right at the top point of the border between the British north of Ireland and Eire. To reach our prayer meeting, we borrowed Helene's red mini again and headed towards Strabane, notorious for its disturbances. There we crossed the border and nosed into Donegal.

I don't remember either of us being concerned about the location or the travel in the dark. We just enjoyed telling those farming folk all about Chefoo. Irish hospitality is lavish. Irish people laugh at bedtime *snacks*. Instead at about ten pm you face tables groaning under fresh cream flans, pavlovas, cheese cakes, tray-bakes and everything that makes a missionary return to duty with a weight problem. By the time we'd indulged in all of this and chatted nonstop as though the night were young, we didn't manage to leave Donegal until around midnight.

It was then I began to feel we were in the middle of nowhere. All the horrific tales of the IRA's border activities made the hair on the back of my neck stand on end. If only the night weren't so black ... If only there was more traffic on the road ... If only we were home ...

My uneasiness grew as we realized the police had thrown a cordon around Strabane. We skirted the town by an unknown road, not knowing we had avoided — only just — the bombing of a garage on our route.

Strabane behind us, we began to breathe more

freely. But not for long. A red light flashed full centre ahead, swaying to right and left, throwing its gleam ominously on our windscreen. We couldn't see anyone: just the beam in the blackness. But we knew we were being waved down.

*Who* was demanding we should stop? Unfortunately we knew only too well how IRA terrorists stole vehicles for their car bombs.

"What'll I do?" panted John. "Drive through it?"

"John! Better stop! They'll puncture our tyres and maybe us, if we try escaping."

Hearts pounding, we drew the mini to a halt. The lateness of the hour, the eeriness of that country road, made me wonder if this was it. Even worse, I knew it was not fanciful imagination. This was life in Northern Ireland in 1974.

John wound down the window. A torch, not a gun, poked through the space. An Ulster policeman! I have never been so glad to see a bobby in all my life.

"Where are you going at this hour, sir? Where have you been? Car registration number, sir?"

And, horrors, we didn't know the number of Helene's red mini. "I'll need to examine your boot," the policeman said. When he was satisfied that it was full of OMF books (dynamite of a different type) and that our story held together, he let us go. As Londonderry's lights hit the horizon two rather shaken missionaries offered prayers of thanksgiving for their protection.

It was one of home leave's tough times to see Northern Ireland so changed, so bound by terror. Dad, returning from the Gaslight Company on foot one evening, was just about to turn into Clooney Park where we lived, when a soldier dashed up, "Take cover, sir! Immediately!" He had no sooner spok than a bullet whizzed past.

"And yet," declared my mother, "our lives are really lived normally. Visitors to our lovely land are surprised because the media paints such a frightful picture. Underneath, though" she added, "there's a certain sadness that we think this is 'normal life'".

Normal? Normal to see soldiers in town with machine guns, walking in twos and threes, backs to the wall, swivelling constantly in an effort to escape a sniper's bullet?

Normal for John and me to separate in the city centre for frisking in different kiosks before we could proceed with our shopping?

Normal to try the door handle into the Irish linen shop only to find it unyielding until a buzz from inside indicated we'd been vetted and the lock electronically released?

Normal to have a Security Officer at the door of every shop to check your basket for a parcel bomb?

After four years in the safety of Malaysia's jungle, John and I did not think life in Northern Ireland normal. Incessant delays in traffic queues while every vehicle was examined ... The old familiar picture windows of my favourite shops boarded up ... It seemed unreal. Where was our beautiful city set on a hill, of the sixties?

As autumn slipped into winter we began to relax as we crossed the Irish Sea again. Our deputation tour was now taking us to unfamiliar territory.

Harrogate, Newcastle-upon-Tyne, Darlington, Berwick-on-Tweed. England's North East was cold and damp. The more we talked about Chefoo the more I missed it. By that time too, I was longing to get back to *Hey There* and Jonathan. I began to wonder if my most dreaded thing was living out of a suitcase and sleeping in five different beds in one week. Yet by November we made it. November — the month of the motorway.

But our anticipated joy had only been a mirage. We arrived home to find the bottom falling out of our happy world.

To our consternation Jonathan's opinion of boarding school had drastically altered. That first Sunday back saw storms of tears and a heart full of hang-ups.

Everything we wanted to do for the Lord depended on Jonathan settling at school. That weekend we discovered he hadn't. And it didn't look as though he was going to either. He wasn't in favour of going back — even for one more week.

"But ... " I said weakly. But the "but" stayed.

Then came prayers that were more fervent than we'd ever prayed for his school uniform. "Lord, please may he settle. We've promised Chefoo we'd go back. We'd like to go back but we just can't leave Jonathan like this."

"Give him time," said John, but he was worried, too. It seemed as though we'd reached the first real crisis point in our missionary lives.

On Sundays we brought J-boy home for the day. Sometimes we filled the car with his friends. We'd plan coffee breaks en route by the lake of mallards. We tracked positives, followed all his negatives, let him talk it out, explained, "But, you see ..."; yet he still went back to school in tears.

"Jonathan, tell you what we'll do! We'll go to Ireland for Christmas! You can sleep in your old nursery in *Heatherlea*. It will be like old times and when you come back, things will be different. You'll be a second-termer then — not a new boy any longer."

As the lark in the family surfaced these weeks, it

was dark — winter dark. And it was cold. Very early in the morning I'd settle in Richard's big leather armchair with black coffee and The Song of Solomon. In the glow of the gas fire, I handled this precious volume that was my Bible. I felt just the way Annabel had expressed it at one of our Camerons' Ladies Bible Groups. "Do you ever feel," she asked "that you can't quite get enough of it?" These early hours were the highlight of my day.

Hudson Taylor, whose commentary *Union and Communion* I was following, said that The Song of Solomon was a poem describing the life of a believer on earth. "Are we not all too apt," he asked, "to seek God rather because of our need than for His joy and pleasure?"

*Hold on!* I thought, *Do you mean God actually has joy and pleasure in me? Impossible!*

My approach to the Lord generally was an apologetic one. I was for ever making so many mistakes.

It was then I heard King Solomon's words like the very voice of the Lord Jesus:

"My lover spoke and said to me,
        'Arise my darling,
    my beautiful one, and come with me'"

Hesitatingly, wondering if the heavenly Bridegroom could possibly mean me, I reached out to follow. Was He really saying, "How beautiful you are, my darling! Oh, how beautiful! ... Come with me from Lebanon, my bride, come with me ... You have stolen my heart... How delightful is your love, my sister, my bride!"?

As the poem became more meaningful, reinforcing to me the love the Lord Jesus had demonstrated at Calvary, I tried to respond like the bride in the story, "Draw me after You and let us run together". Up and down the mountains of spices I sped, immersed in this new picture of Christ's love for me. It was suddenly like being aware of self-worth. I felt cradled in His "much desired shade". I learned my favourite parts to make sure I remembered He'd said that about me. Then and often since, the Song of Solomon has been my favourite Bible book because it makes me feel like a princess.

"Heavenly Bridegroom," I whispered from the brown leather, "what shall we do about our problem? Is it right for us, the Miller family, to go through with separation from each other? Jesus Lover of my soul, could You let me know soon? It affects our whole future."

At breakfast times too, John and I would linger over *Hey There's* breakfast bar using a book of devotional readings — "Hudson Taylor's Legacy". Silence descended on the kitchen the morning we read "Who were the Losers?" A silence that stole over even our perturbed prayers for Jonathan.

*"He that withholdeth corn, the people shall curse him: but blessing shall be upon the head of him that selleth it"* (Proverbs 11: 26).

"The disciples began to think that Jesus *meant* what He *said; and they acted on His directions.* They began to love as brethren; to sell that which they had, and give alms. No member of the Church had any lack. Doubtless many of the wise ones of this world spoke scornfully of such fanaticism, and folly, and prided themselves on their own possessions, determining to 'leave the rest of their substance to their babes.' But *did they do so*?

"A few years rolled on, and, as foretold by the Master, troublous times came. Jerusalem was compassed with armies. *The day for selling possessions and using the proceeds for Jesus was passed.*

"Who were the losers? ... some members of the Church, perhaps, abode by their stuff in Jerusalem, instead of fleeing to the mountains. Again I ask: *Who were the losers?*"

"Our missionary service hasn't cost us very much up until now," I observed, breaking the silence.

My mind was full of Jonathan's unhappiness but John was thinking of something else.

"'Blessing shall be upon the head of him that selleth'," he repeated. "Sheila, are you thinking the same thoughts as I am?"

Quite suddenly, I was.

"We've never burnt our boats behind us," John stated. "Everything's been very easy."

"Up until this point," I put in.

"Well?"

My elbow leaned on the breakfast bar and I cradled my head in one hand. A tear slid sideways into my hair.

*Heatherlea*! My security blanket.

"You want to sell the house?" I whispered.

"'Who were the losers?'" quoted John.

In my mind's eye I saw our ties to a "normal" life being snatched away. Jonathan, our only child — and now *Heatherlea*. I thought I just couldn't take it. I couldn't see a spectrum of colour through my tears. I couldn't trace any rainbows.

"Sheila, let's pray about this specifically. Perhaps when we go over to Ireland for Christmas, we should fix up *Heatherlea* FOR SALE."

# Christmas is Really For the Children

Christmas is really
for the children.
Especially for children
who like animals, stables,
stars and babies wrapped
in swaddling clothes.
Then there are wise men,
kings in fine robes,
humble shepherds and a
hint of rich perfume.

There is also room
for the children
unless accompanied by a
grown-up boy
who has neither blind faith
or apparent allegiance
of being a Christian.
It employs politics, cash
and the arms of the world.
It is too good for people
of religious disposition.
That is why we listen to
think on why it's Christmas
and the first member of
of course.

Or they've got better
and I'm in terror of
Christmas without asking
too many questions about
what Jesus did when he grew up
or whether there's any connection.

Steve Turner

# Christmas is Really For the Children

Christmas is really
for the children.
Especially for children
who like animals, stables,
stars and babies wrapped
in swaddling clothes.
Then there are wise men,
kings in fine robes,
humble shepherds and a
hint of rich perfume.

Easter is not really
for the children
unless accompanied by a
cream filled egg.
It has whips, blood, nails,
a spear and allegations
of body snatching.
It involves politics, God
and the sins of the world.
It is not good for people
of nervous disposition.
They would do better to
think on rabbits, chickens
and the first snowdrop
of spring.
Or they'd do better to
wait for a re-run of
Christmas without asking
too many questions about
what Jesus did when he grew up
or whether there's any connection.

*Steve Turner*

# 13

# Winter in Monochrome

That winter, colour faded out of life for me. 1975 emerged from a time tank of despair like an underexposed photograph.

Our decision to visit Ireland was double-pronged. John's left ear was causing concern again. The ENT Consultant in Belfast told him he would need further surgery.

"There's a new operation, you know," the specialist, world renowned, explained. "Tympanoplasty. I could do a middle-ear reconstruction and repair your perforated ear-drum. And, in fact, there'd be a 75% chance of restoration of hearing."

All our eyes shining at this prospect, John admitted himself to the Royal Victoria Hospital, situated in the no-man's land between the now infamous Shankill and Falls Roads.

But the miracle didn't happen.

Was it because of our second reason that John's ear didn't heal, quite apart from the hearing? We had decided to put *Heatherlea* on the market. John plunged into all that the sale involved too soon after surgery.

We painted walls, shampooed carpets, washed the grimy venetian blinds, made the fridge and oven usable again; we had our elegant dining room table french polished because one resident had used it as an ironing board. Although J-boy thought *Heatherlea* resembled a doll's house after living in *Hey There*, we were agreed it looked so good that we'd like to live in it ourselves.

But the shadow of that impossibility was hanging over the three of us like a Damoclean Sword.

Instead, only days after surgery, John was loading the Avenger over and over again in the January snow, the collar of his winter coat turned up to protect his ear.

January 8 was John's birthday. John, being John, and gifted with an unquenchable sense of humour, had prepared for this great event as far back as November. The following letter had been posted to Chefoo for the Staff Bulletin Board.

"Dear Comrades,

I just want to remind you that my birthday is coming up in January. Heavy parcels such as Malaysian pewter or batik shirts should be mailed soon to avoid the Christmas rush. Smaller, more costly items, like gold tie-clips, would be better sent airmail as would cheques, postal orders or currency notes. These can be posted after Christmas.

Keep the action going.

We'll be back soon,
John"

Loyal to the upward turn of their merry mouths, they sent a package. A man-sized apron. Two-inch-high staff signatures in bright-hued laundry ink decorated the front. The waist bands bore the inscription "We're all tied to your apron strings"! That apron is one of our stored away treasures. I encouraged John to try it out frequently — but he seemed reluctant to do so somehow. "Too precious," he said with a straight face.

In actual fact, the eighth of January was celebrated by driving to Dublin to put Jonathan on a plane for school. My special cousin Natalie, married to a pilot, just "happened" to live in Bath. She was going to meet Jonathan in Bristol.

"Mr McDonagh rang when you were at the airport," my mother reported on our return. "He wanted news of you. He wondered why the Lord had laid the three of you on his heart all day." David and Helene McDonagh headed up the OMF Council in Northern Ireland.

Hudson Taylor had said about the beautiful text in the book of Ruth — "'... under whose wings thou art come to trust': If it is sometimes dark, the shadow is but the shadow of His wings."

*But what about Jonathan?* I thought. *I can feel the dark. I'm in a tunnel. But my tunnel is dark because his is.* Thomas a Kempis had written, "All Christ's life was a cross and martyrdom; and thou seekest to thyself rest and joy?" And I knew the Bible taught that we must "endure" suffering but — no one seemed to be able to answer my query, *What if that suffering involves another person?* I thought I could cope with my own tunnel but I couldn't take it if Jonathan continued to go through his.

*Heatherlea* now ready for viewers, John and I tackled our memories stored in the roof space. Out went J-boy's baby clothes, decorations from our wedding cake, my veil, my "Mother" magazines. Nostalgia washed over me like a North Atlantic breaker. If only I could live at *Heatherlea* again with my precious baby, my toddler.

Those eight weeks in Ireland were a sorry ordeal. Worst of all — I couldn't take what was happening in my stride. Was it only a few months previously that I sang over the problem of buying Jonathan's uniform? When Scripture in Song cassettes turned *Hey There's* kitchen into a temple of worship? What happened to the lessons I'd learned through *Power in Praise*? It was King Alfred the Great who said, "If thou hast a fearful thought, share it not with a weakling, whisper it to thy saddle-bow, and ride forth singing." Now, in winter, I failed totally to get on top of our circumstances. I never felt like singing and my ideas on "mindset" eluded me.

Strange how I'd only felt homesick at Christmas time in Chefoo's valley. Now, all I wanted was to get back, to recapture happiness, to forget this trail of despair. Amy Carmichael (following Bishop Moule) called times like these "occasions for victory". Well, I missed it.

But one day, the Larne-Stranraer ferry landed us in Scotland. A touch of spring was in the air and a pale sun shone with a ray of hope. As we coasted south Jonathan's bicycle, tied to the roof rack, cast a happy shadow on the hedgerows. And on our arrival in the South West, we found his weekly missive positive and full of high spirits. He'd enclosed a "Peanuts". "Is this appropriate to you, Mum?" he asked. His sense of humour was a life-saver. Snoopy had his nose in a letter. "Dear Contributor, Thank you for submitting your story to our magazine. To save time we are enclosing two rejection slips ... " Snoopy collapsed on his kennel top and typewriter for the punchline "... one for this story and one for the next story you send us!"

February was earmarked for study. Before we'd ever headed East, John had started work on psychology at London University. He had arranged with OMF to use some of his home-leave months to get his degree.

"How can you cram three years' work into six months?" I wanted to know.

The lady at Birkbeck College who decided such things said the same. The university was running two courses in Practical Psychology after each other — one for second-year students, one for third. John applied for both.

"Impossible," said this lady who knew about things like that. "Next year, come back and do the Advanced Course."

But next year John would be in Malaysia. He felt almost too discouraged to appeal against the decision.

It was as if the Lord was saying, "Leave it to me." Incredibly John was given permission to attend both courses and to sit his final exams in June. He had determination, concentration and a retentive memory going for him.

How keen he was to get at those books. And he did, despite further missionary conferences in March and a trip to Ireland for after-care treatment for his ear.

I was high with excitement the night he flew in again from the Emerald Isle. He brought my sister back with him. Adeline, who had lost her teddy bear at the Children's Special Service Mission when she was three!

Adeline had grown up bubbling over with life and full of fun. She was a superb mimic. When she and our old friend Cecil got together, doing take offs on the Irish, we howled with laughter.

But this Adeline who accompanied John was different. Life had dealt her some severe blows.

Already she had two broken marriages behind her and was making an effort to bring up four children on her own.

It was when I was reading Isaiah 58 about how to fast properly, thinking of healing for John's ear, I came across verse 7. "Is not this the kind of fasting I have chosen ... not to turn away from your own flesh and blood?"

Adeline. My mind had filled with thoughts of Adeline.

*She's had it very rough. But what can I do*, I wondered? Would a holiday over here help her? How could she leave her family to come across, though?

But with the help of my mother, we got it all arranged. *Hey There's* hymns of praise began to help restore my sister's battered spirit. But I could see she was far from well ...

John's studies in psychology did not help in my concern for Adeline. He, too, could see she was plumbing depths we were unable to reach with her. Nor could his text books help me in my dilemma about leaving Jonathan at boarding school. Parental deprivation could affect children adversely. The more we visited Monkton Combe Junior School, the more I fell in love with it. I could see J-boy would have a superb education there — more so than we could ever have provided in Ireland. Jonathan thought it was a good school too, but couldn't he be a *day* boy?

I don't think I've ever prayed for anything so much as for confirmation from the Lord that we were on the right track in sending him there *and then going away*.

Friends made comforting noises. They quoted that favourite text to me about leaving home and family for the Lord's sake and receiving a hundred-fold in return. But it didn't meet my need at that point. I could see all that. It applied to us. But nobody seemed to be able to reassure me on the issue of what we were doing to our *child*.

One day in desperation, I said to John, "I feel that unless the Lord shows me quite definitely that I must go back to Chefoo, then my first call is to stay at home with Jonathan."

And John replied, "Sheila, the Lord called us to Chefoo. He has never rescinded that call. We can't decide to stay back."

That was the only answer I had.

But the spring months saw me continually pleading with my Heavenly Father that He would show me if Jonathan fell into the category of children who could weather the trauma of parents living eight thousand miles away. There are children and children, I knew. One of our OMF families had three at boarding school but their second child lived at home. The parents were sensitive enough to know that she had a different emotional make-up. Where along the continuum did Jonathan lie?

Too soon June made its debut. *Hey There's* garden and the country roads en route to Bath were reminiscent of Wordsworth's poetry. But the fresh greens of an English summer appeared to me again in faded-photograph perspective. Things were happening too fast. The kind of things that made me gasp for air. Things that robbed my life of colour.

John had word from the Royal Victoria Hospital that the graft on his ear drum had not taken. He would need further surgery.

"Our flight to Kuala Lumpur has to be postponed until September," explained John. This would mean that Jonathan couldn't come with us. The promise of going to Malaysia for the summer had been like a dangling carrot to the three of us for Jonathan's heart was in the mountains where he had done most of his growing up.

These new arrangements added the complication that we had nowhere to go between July and September. Our year in *Hey There* was up. Richard and Helen were due home.

My mother got in touch and in a worried tone divulged the news that Adeline was in hospital

John took himself off to London, amid all our problems, to sit his finals — six hours every day for five days.

Jonathan completed his first year at Monkton Combe Junior School with an excellent report, especially in Art and English. Too bad his Social Studies' master had written "There are great gaps in his knowledge of British Geography". I'd been the one responsible for teaching the British Isles at Chefoo so I didn't take to that too kindly!

Then the three of us packed. We moved to OMF's wellknown Headquarters in London: Newington Green. A heatwave hit London that summer. The nineteenth-century brick guest house was smothered in it like a claustrophobic blanket; oppressive, stifling; especially the telephone kiosk in the hall. I used to wedge my foot in the self-closing door to exchange the fetid air for sultry.

But one morning it didn't matter any more what the air was like in there. The mission home hostess hurriedly climbed several flights of polished stairs — early.

"Sheila," she called, "are you awake? Can you come for a long-distance telephone call?"

It was my mother. Adeline was dead.

I ran from the call-box. I ran towards that cassette recorder which allegorized my life. I wanted the fast-forward button. I wanted to go back to Chefoo, where life had been all sunshine ...

## Parting from my Son

*The plane wheels lurch, leave*
*the tarmac, tightening*
*the inescapable cord.*
                    *The tug*
*brings sudden tears. No use to call myself*
*a fool. Time has no help for*
*what ails me.*

*Son, grown to a colossus, striding*
*the streets in your high boots, spinning*
*your gaudy fantasies,*
*your desperado moustache is*
*no disguise to me.*

*I leave you where the wind*
*blows cold off the river and*

*your dreams are not enough*
*to keep me warm.*

                    *Evangeline Paterson*

# 14

# *The White Witch*

I t was one of those afternoons at Chefoo when knitting-needles of rain stabbed the valley with tropical fury. The playing field was a quagmire; the wide drains gushed like topaz rapids; flights of steps to our mountain homes were waterfalls and the children were dormitory-bound, in sweaters, waiting for their chocolate-coloured baths.

"This place is nothing but a green bucket!" declared Barry.

I was quite horrified.

Barry was the new eligible bachelor from New Zealand who'd joined the teaching staff. *If you lived in Ireland,* I thought, *you'd find it never rains itself out. But here! Why, tomorrow morning the sky will be blue again.*

A green bucket? To me the valley was a hanging basket, cradled between Mount Jasar and Mount Brinchang with blessings sliding down the mountain sides from the Heavenly Gardener Himself; guarded by mighty warrior angels from the clear sky above.

In fact, it was said that the skies in the Camerons were so singular in their beauty that experts came from many places in the world to study the cloud formations. So someone said.

"And," said Barry, "the bucket has a lid. A grey one."

Strange, I'd never noticed such greyness before. For four years the valley had been bathed in sunshine. We all knew about the white witch, of course. When she descended, we ran for shelter. A downpour was preceded by swirling mists racing down the mountain slopes, shrouding the school.

"It nervouses me," said Debbie, "The white witch."

Never before had there been a tug-of-war somewhere inside me about Chefoo. I felt, heard, saw, touched, thought sunshine, cobalt skies, candy floss clouds, slaty-backed forktails, bulbuls with colouring like parrots, mountain minivets, painted Jezebels and shiny millipedes. But after home leave my emotions were a rope and for a while the tug of the white witch won.

August 4 had seen a brief but traumatic entry in my diary, written at Newington Green:

"Heard of Adeline's death today: Tragically she slept all her troubles away.

"Also heard today that John had gained his Honours Degree in Psychology at London University.

"Our flight date is September 7."

It had been a rather dazed trio who walked to Birkbeck College to see the graduates' results pinned on the big glass-covered notice board. Our congratulations for John were clouded with the business of trying to live among the dying.

I remember comforting my mother. Strangled words, "It's best, Mummy. She wasn't able to go on. It's worse for you because you were the one who just kept on loving her. I was a mere onlooker. I couldn't comprehend the depth of her despair..."

"But it was our wedding anniversary ...," she wept.

On the day of Adeline's funeral, I had stared at my swollen eyes in the Newington Green bedroom mirror.

"We have a little sister," I said to the mirror. "What shall we do for our sister?"

The words had been with me all day. Familiar. What were they? Where did they come from? "We have a little sister ... " How apposite. How strange the way they lingered in my mind.

Suddenly the mirror reflected the answer. "Remember? *Hey There*. The Song of Solomon — when life was happy in the brown leather armchair."

"We have a little sister ... What shall we do for our sister?"

I didn't know. But if the Bible asked the question, maybe it gave an answer. Hurriedly I leafed through the pages.

"We have a little sister ... " Yes, there it was. "If she be a door we will enclose her with boards ... "

At that very moment Adeline was lying in her coffin. "Oh God," I moaned, "it's true. She is enclosed with boards. What does it mean?"

After a hunt the crumpled red paper-back "Union and Communion" came to light, and surely the Lord spoke through Hudson Taylor's words:

"... if (she) is unstable and easily moved to and fro like a door ... she will need to be enclosed with boards of cedar, hedged in with restraints, for her own protection."

*For her own protection* That was it. Had much greater tragedy been averted? "For her own protection". I began to understand.

Adeline's children were collected by their respective fathers. *Our* child went to his hostel parents. With shadows like bruises under my eyes, John and I returned to Malaysia.

Sometimes I wonder why the Lord bothers with us. Despite my yo-yo efforts to follow the heavenly Bridegroom, He acted as the true Lover of my soul before we boarded that Boeing 747.

At five minutes to midnight, he answered my prayers about Jonathan.

His method was a love-letter from Himself but written by Betty. Betty was the authoress who started me pen-pushing in the sixties after my surgery. "Therapeutic, Sheila," she had insisted. "Don't say you can't. Say 'If God wants me to, I'll try.'" We were still in touch. She was one with whom I'd shared my lack of peace.

On September 5 her letter arrived. Perhaps it is truer to say at *one* minute to midnight.

Twice God had prompted Betty to send an Amy Carmichael poem. "As I thought of this prayer," she wrote, "the 'I' changed to 'they' and I found it a far more piercing word. I was not sure if I could pray it for my children." I knew she was thinking of the masculine pronoun for me.

"From prayer that asks that 'he' may be
Sheltered from winds that beat on Thee,
From fearing when 'he' should aspire
From faltering when 'he' should climb higher,
From silken self. O Captain, free
Thy soldier who would follow Thee.

"Then I thought of the angels watching our Lord Jesus as He walked the roads of the earth," continued Betty, "beaten by winds — and what bitter winds! Did they ever come to the Father with pitiful prayers for His shelter? Would they have made it harder for that Father ... by asking Him to do what He could not do without eternal loss to His beloved Son and the souls that He had made?"

What is insight? How can I use words to explain the bright flash of perception that was suddenly mine in that Newington Green hall. The blue pages of the letter fluttered in my hand. "John," I breathed, "God has sent me my answer."

I had been willing to hand a happy contented son over to the Lord. It had never occurred to me that God might *want* winds to blow on Jonathan, to buffet Jonathan, in order to shape his character. The maternal, over-protective instinct that was part of me had been determined to shield Jonathan from any wind I could find — homesickness, loneliness, parental deprivation — the lot.

And that morning I suddenly saw that when God gave His only Son, He gave Him to *un*happiness.

I'd never seen it like that before. I needed to love Jonathan enough to hand him over to the Lord for the life He saw right for our twelve-year-old.

All at one minute to midnight.

This new perspective did not *mean* a joyful farewell. But it brought peace.

A few days later other mothers' sacrifices sang a welcome song to greet us, "When the Millers come marching home ..." Home. The hanging-basket-valley that became a green bucket.

*At Hey There*, I had had two possible sedatives in mind when praying for Jonathan:

1) "Lord, if only I could know that this is what you want for him ..." Now I believed the Lord had given me that remedial treatment.

2) "Lord, if only Jonathan wasn't going through a

tunnel of despair, then I wouldn't be. I'd be all right ..."
Now the Malay postman on his red motorbike began
to bring us all sorts of cheering news. J-boy had come
second in a Scripture essay. He was first in some
science scholarship quiz which won his name an entry
in the Head's "Golden Book". His dorm had been
presented with the shield for high marks. To this day,
I don't know what the "high marks" were for.
Couldn't have been orderliness. He was studying
Architecture in Bath. "Dad," he wrote, as he
approached his 13th birthday, "My birthday brainwave is: — What about a combined birthday and
Christmas present of half a set of golf clubs for the
holidays. See what you think. Mention this to our Mrs
World!"

Anyone could see, even without contact lenses,
that chinks of light were beginning to brighten
Jonathan's tunnel.

Did that mean, as I thought it would, that my own
tunnel was no more? Fond thought!

You see there was THE BOOK. This was OMF's
newest assignment for me. 1981 was going to be
Centennial Year for the Chefoo Schools. A century
since Hudson Taylor had seen the need for a school to
educate the children of missionaries in the land of
their adoption. Building started in Chefoo, China, a
port on the Yellow Sea, and although everything else
was left behind when Communist rule took over, the
missionaries brought the name with them to
Malaysia. "Wouldn't it be good to have a history
dating right back to China days," the Directors asked,
"relating all God's provision for our children through
one hundred years? You'd be the obvious one to try it,
Sheila."

In a moment of naivety I had said, "Yes".

In anticipation of this mammoth task, John had helped me to compile a questionnaire at *Hey There*. We posted these out all over the world. They arrived in the homes of Chefusians everywhere — young Chefusians, middle-aged Chefusians, the elderly, the fond-happy-memories type, the jolly-take-life-as-it-comes type. But the questionnaire also found those who blamed every hang-up they'd ever had on being sent to boarding school.

In the preface of the finished manuscript I eventually wrote, "The global response was tremendous — filled-in forms, closely written sheets of reminiscences, ancient diaries, photographs, sketches, old magazines, cuttings from newspapers, manuscripts and even cassette tapes. I felt totally inadequate for the assignment OMF had asked me to undertake ... Bishop Frank Houghton summed up my trepidation in these lovely words:

'It is a secret joy
    to find
    The task assigned
Beyond our powers,
    For then, if ought of good be wrought,
    Clearly the praise is His
    Not ours!'"

The task assigned sure was beyond my powers. One lady wrote asking how anybody who'd never been to China could write about the school there. Soon I was floundering in a sea of research, my day's teaching, the frequent entertaining plus all the little extras that fell into the lap of the headmaster's wife.

One evening as I set the table for supper with places for several families, I thought, "I can't go on. I'm too tired. How far can one push one's body? There's tomorrow evening as well." But I knew I *would* carry it through and wondered why I couldn't express my weariness by dramatically fainting — flat and cold on the Assembly Hall floor with everyone there!

John rearranged my timetable to help. I taught Creative English and French part time for some months.

And the letters kept coming — cheery letters, funny ones, missives chapter-length and ... the dreadful.

The "dreadful" became the dreaded.

"I feel as though I was sacrificed on the altar of my parents' missionary career."

"There was a strange man thousands of miles away who was my father ..."

"My parents deserted me at an age when I needed them."

"The deprivation was often to such a degree as to be crippling for life."

Could accusations like these really be written about Chefoo School, China? How would I handle info like this? Should it go in the book? Already letters were asking for a story that wasn't pure saccharine.

But a second source of anxiety outdid the first. The censures pointed to something deeper. How could I cope with the possibility that we, John and I, had set out on a course of action that would cause Jonathan to feel the same way?

"John," I exclaimed, "these letters are driving me round the bend."

"All of them?"

"No. Of course not! But listen to this. It's neurotic. No. It's *psy*chotic. 'Who am I? Just a number. 271' What if Jonathan is affected like this? The responses to our questionnaire, lying on this desk, show that people have been psychologically bruised by being sent to boarding school."

"How do you know their maladjustment is due to boarding school?" asked John. "Maybe they were maladjusted people anyway."

"Here's another," I cried. "'The trauma of separation from families was devastating. Whatever we gained academically was certainly lost psychologically!'"

"There are families and families," stated John. "Could have been a good thing for *lots* of children to be brought up at boarding school. That way they escaped the mistakes of their parents."

"John! You've studied this subject. Can't you see we might be damaging Jonathan psychologically?"

Think of all the kids who *have* stayed at home;" pointed out John, "children who have grown up with caring Christian backgrounds but they didn't make it in life either. *They* can't blame boarding school on their lapses. How does anyone know that boarding school has caused all their hang ups?"

"But ... *Jonathan* ...?" I persisted.

"Sheila, Jonathan is a well-adjusted, reasonably happy teenager. He knows he's secure in our love for him. If we find in the holidays that he's not taking life in his stride, we'll all talk it over together and make new plans. Perhaps he'd like to go to Faith Academy in the Philippines. It would mean an American education for a British child but — he'd be nearer."

Then John came out with one of those insightful questions of his. "Have you weighed up these negative letters against all your positive replies?"

"No."

"Well, perhaps you're being economical with the truth, then. We'd better get going on some statistics."

The record was set straight in the chapter "Thorn Bushes Have Roses" in the Centennial Anthology, *Pigtails, Petticoats and the Old School Tie* and as I read the fun letters, I saw it was me, not Jonathan, who wasn't taking life in stride.

I began to lose weight. My mouth didn't seem to turn up at the corners like it used to. My tight expression hid pained thoughts.

Jonathan boarding the jet at Kuala Lumpur's airport after Christmas. Barely thirteen. Crossing the world on his own because we'd sold *Heatherlea* and had money to pay for his fare. A cine film we took played the reel round and round in my mind. He'd waved his tennis racquet from the cabin hatchway. Then the grey, steel prison leaped into life, speeding him away from me. I'd peered into the evening sky until the full stop representing it, wasn't there any more. *Life is at a full stop. Period.* I thought That night I made myself ill, crying. After Jonathan had left, of course. Even though his golf clubs were lovingly awaiting the summer.

My mother and father came to see Chefoo — something I'd longed for since the beginning of this adventure with God. But somehow I couldn't enter into the potential joy their visit should have brought.

I had one lifeline and I clung to it desperately. The blue letter from Betty. God had made it clear to me in the Newington Green hallway that this was the way forward for the Miller Trio. "Lord, what's wrong with me then?" I cried.

The skies were not like brass. It was not a "dark-night-of-the-soul" experience. God was there. Accessible. With me in it all. He cradled me, nurtured me, had me sing, showed me Philemon verse 15, "Perhaps this is why he was parted from you for a little while, that you might have him back for ever ..." as a son in the Lord, I thought, so that we'd all be in heaven together. If ever the words of a hymn were true for me then, it was the one about your anchor holding in the storms of life.

But a year after we'd returned to the green bucket, I climbed into the jet *with* Jonathan. "Nervous exhaustion," Dr Monica had said. She had taken me to see Professor Khoo in Singapore. "Home rest" was the prescription.

As Ireland was more tense than I was, Áberdeen in Scotland was to be my home for four months. Mr and Mrs Roworth, Jonathan's godparents, braved this onslaught.

Margaret, one of Malaysia's missionaries, had shown me a beautiful promise in my hymnbook.

> "Green pastures are before me
> which yet I have not seen;
> Bright skies will soon be o'er me,
> where the dark clouds have been."

I had read in Exodus how the Israelis "came to Elim where there were twelve springs and seventy palm trees." But Mrs Roworth asked me if I'd settle for a fountain and a very healthy rubber plant!

Just to be on the same island as our offspring got the period of rest going with a bang, not a whimper.

# No Scar

*Hast thou no scar?*
*No hidden scar on foot, or side, or hand?*
*I hear thee sung as mighty in the land,*
*I hear them hail thy bright ascendant star,*
*Hast thou no scar?*

*Hast thou no wound?*
*Yet I was wounded by the archers, spent,*
*Leaned Me against a tree to die; and rent*
*By ravening beasts that compassed Me, I swooned:*
*Hast thou no wound?*

*No wound? no scar?*
*Yet, as the Master shall the servant be,*
*And piercèd are the feet that follow Me;*
*But thine are whole: can he have followed far*
*Who has nor wound nor scar?*

Amy Carmichael

# 15

# Colour me beautiful

Life ricocheted from the sublime to the ridiculous in Aberdeen. Tears and laughter. Disquiet and delight.

Mr Carr arrived mid-stage. He was OMF's Home Director then. Mr Carr is a dear teddy-bear of a man. I always feel at ease with him. But his advice held nothing of the soft cuddly toy variety. His message was clear. His words strong.

"Why don't you cut the apron strings, Sheila?" he asked.

I was totally taken aback.

How could anyone think a missionary mother kept her son on apron strings? Hadn't I proved they'd been axed by living eight thousand miles away? I really was quite astounded.

"Sheila, last September you made an initial act of surrendering Jonathan to God. Now, a year later, you need to daily acknowledge that decision."

The silken-self-feeling began to come into focus. Amy Carmichael's description of the pair of us — Jonathan and me.

"Are you yearning after him like the Israelis looked back to Egypt from the desert? They had made the decision to leave home for God."

I swallowed hard.

"Look at Scripture, Sheila," Mr Carr pressed on. A gentle gentleman with relentless words. "Joseph was smothered by the love of his father. God *let* the brothers get rid of Joseph. Extraordinary at the time but see it with hindsight."

The silken-self-feeling started to back off.

"Think of David. A child when his mother had to let him go. I'm sure she would have wanted to spare him his problems with Saul.

"Do you want Jonathan to turn into a jellyfish?" pursued Mr Carr. "God loves Jonathan as much as he did Joseph. God was preparing Joseph for his life's work. If Jacob had kept his hands on him, what then?"

I took the point. Hands off. Remarkable that Mr Carr had echoed Betty's blue letter.

"Oh," I sighed later to dear Mr Roworth, "I find it so hard to give up the rights of motherhood!"

Perhaps I expected him to hand me a hankie; to put a comforting arm round my shoulders. I certainly thought he would gentle me somehow.

Instead Mr Roworth said, "What rights, Sheila?"

The silken-self-feeling curled up like a worm.

It was then I really saw it. Saw *them*. Two principles. "Your attitude should be the kind that was shown us by Christ Jesus," wrote Paul to the Philippians, "who, though he was God, did not demand and cling to his rights..." It was as though the Lord Jesus was sitting there in Person reminding me that He had once said, "A servant is not above his master."

"And," explained Mr R, "Jonathan was given to you as a *gift*. A life to hold in trust. He's *God's* creation."

So. I had no rights. No rights at all.

A few weeks passed and, feeling desperately low, I went to bed early one night. But not to fall asleep. In the dark I couldn't see the pretty checked yellow curtains. I couldn't even feel the comfort of the matching continental quilt. My eyes felt stretched and dry. Locked up inside me was all my despair.

*When am I ever going to snap out of this?* I said to myself. *I've accepted these points about motherhood but I reckon that, besides missing Jonathan, I'm miserable anyway. Where is my usual happy, optimistic, enthusiastic self?*

Pessimism replied. "Perhaps you're not going to snap out of it. Perhaps you're on the brink of a nervous breakdown. It's a very fine line, you know, between nervous exhaustion and total breakdown."

There didn't seem to be any moon that night. The bedroom was so black.

*That's it*, I thought. *I'm just like Adeline. Adeline who couldn't cope with life.*

It was an easy leap to the next speculation. *Surely it couldn't run in the family. Could it?*

Adeline had died. Would I be forced to give up too?

The blackness was almost tangible.

And then ... like a missile, it came to me what was happening. A ray of enlightenment lit the source of such thinking.

Satan.

Dr Monica in Singapore had lent me a book before I'd flown home. With her cognizance she had foreseen the devil having a heyday with me. The book taught how to take authority over him in the name of the Lord Jesus.

I had a dread of Satan but, knowing he was a conquered enemy, I gathered the dregs of my courage and spoke softly into the black night.

"Satan, I only dare to address you covered with the protective blood of the Lord Jesus. In His name, I tell you to get out of my mind, out of my thinking, out of this room. I trust in the Lord Jesus. You did your worst to Him at Calvary and it didn't come off. *He's* the Victor and one day you'll be left in your own hell.

"Father God," I whispered next, "I commit myself to you for protection."

And out of the tunnel came words that I hadn't sung since *Hey There* days. I knew this song couldn't suddenly have come to mind all by itself, as I had a new repertoire now.

Into the dusk I sang,
"I shall not die
But I shall live
To praise Thy Name, O Lord".

The despair faded. In its place came a sense of the Lord's presence. No bright shaft of light slanted through the room. Just a quiet peace in the darkness. A miracle. And with His reassurance I was able to continue picking up in health.

Missing John was the worst part of being in Britain for autumn, but he kept me on the receiving end of happy letters and cassettes. The staff at Chefoo was only half there! I mean by this that a widespread changeover had taken place since our halcyon prefurlough days. No Cynthia now. "But," said John, "we're working together again as a team." John was right on top and I thought it was a precious spin-off from the Lord in my absence.

John knows how to handle me and has no knots to untie, as I have, with a low self-image. Despite my repeated declarations that his singing is too loud, too regimented and too flat, he chose to render his own version of

"Visions of you
In shades of blue ..." on tape.
Mrs R and I laughed as he came up with
"Visions I trust
In shades of rust ..."!

It meant he wasn't dismayed that I'd splurged on winter clothes in the new season's colour. Neither was the Lord. Having had to spend what I thought was an exorbitant amount for a short cape, I was worrying like mad about stewardship. Just at that point the Lord showed me Matthew 7 in a totally new light. "... don't worry at all about having enough ... clothing ... your Heavenly Father knows perfectly well that you need them." For the first time the lilies of the field didn't condemn me. I was assured God understood.

John came home for Christmas. Mr and Mrs R gave the Miller Trio a relaxed and memorable time of togetherness. Jonathan's trunk from school followed him almost the length of Great Britain. Mrs Roworth and I released the locks in her elegant hall.

We gasped, gulped for air and retreated. Then John and J-boy carried the trunk, with its lid down, to the frozen wastes of the Aberdeen garage. John's free hand was clamped to his nose where his fingers acted like a clothes peg.

The sports' gear from J-boy's last rugger game was bundled in there — unwashed. As I tackled that trunk I grinned up my own sleeve at the new young missionary at Language Centre almost seven years before. The day Mr Heimbach had spoken on commit-ment. All she had wanted to do in life was be a housewife and wash Jonathan's rugby togs. At Christmas 1976, she changed her mind.

I also changed my mind in another area that I thought was "all I wanted in life"! This is where the ridiculous threatened to submerge the sublime. Or should I say the "different" threatened the sublime, because in the end God programmed a new lesson into my life?

By 1976 just about any woman who knew *anything* about fashion was having her ears pierced. It hit me, like finding the treasure at the end of a tracking sortie, that I could get on the band wagon. I was free from my childhood's do's and don'ts and, of course, there was no harm anyway, positively no harm that is, in having one's ears pierced.

I don't know when one of my ideas set me going with such rapture. In my enthusiasm, I was radiating excitement at the thought of having gems in my ears. If there was ever any niggle of doubt left in my mind about the rightness of my new decision it was easy to dismiss. Hadn't I decided to wear lipstick for instance, for the sake of the gospel in *Heatherlea* days? So that I wouldn't look utterly "other" to my fashionable neighbours.

Hadn't Lorraine confided in the Camerons, "You know, Sheila, one thing that made me want to know about you and your Christianity was that you looked sort of normal. You even wore make-up!"

In OMF hadn't I discovered that I'd worn blinkers for years and that they were cultural, not biblical? One of our favourite stories told of a well-known speaker and his bunch of American delegates arriving in the Netherlands for a conference. As the Dutch members of committee viewed askance the feminine visitors, they were shocked to see their painted faces. So shocked that the cigarettes nearly fell out of their mouths.

And didn't Diane and Molly and Margie and a host of others at Chefoo wear ear-rings? Spiritual girls if ever there were any. I even knew OMF directors' wives with pierced ears.

So I thoroughly dwelt in thought on the image that was to be the new me. What fun it would be searching for sets just the right colour to match different outfits. I'd have access to little ones which breathed the mystic east, like minute Chinese characters encircled in gold. Why, I might even be daring enough to try golden hoops — small ones, of course — and when I'd shake my head they'd bang against my cheeks. They'd just improve me so much.

Once I did have a deliberate check on these reflections during my Quiet Time when I found I couldn't justify tampering, even the littlest bit, with how God had created me, that is with no holes in my ear lobes. But if other fine Christians I knew had no qualms about it, need I?

At last I was well enough to arrange the outing to the jewellers. I fingered my lobes and thought how good it was going to be to wiggle round a sleeper or explore a little stud — in just a few hours' time.

"I don't see the point in all this," joked Mr R. "We can't see your ears anyway!"

But I was willing to have my hair cut.

As the appointment drew nearer, I was increasingly aware of a sense of unease spiritually. God had been specially real to me all the time I was ill, and the least little ruffle on the surface of the sea of communication between us made me sensitive to His voice. Each time the niggle of uncertainty stirred, I pushed it down with all my arguments about directors' wives and lovely dorm aunties. And the jewels

I'd wear would be a way to display God's beautiful creativity.

I don't remember ever wanting something quite so much. I really do like to go overboard on my ideas. But the forcefulness of the craving began to make me suspicious. I began to think that if I was to go through with it, I'd better not have a devotional time with my Bible until it was a fait accompli. In my loose-from-restraint type of living I was so loose that I was almost unglued. That thought made my spiritual eyes un-snap. As though the lens cap had dropped from a camera, light glared on my motives. And I saw what was happening.

Was this little affair not really just about ear-rings, nor even the rights or wrongs of wearing them? The sudden clarity made me realize it was something much, much deeper. My mind was set on a thing my old nature desired, as Paul explains it in Romans 8. In the burst of insight I realized nothing was wrong with wearing ear-rings! It was my runaway attitude to them that was the seed-bed for trouble. My vain thoughts were full of the pretty picture I would make wearing jewels in my ears. My imagination had taken me for a ride, and now I began to discern the controlling, chastening hand of a Heavenly Father.

"But, Lord," I pleaded, "you didn't stop my friends, and wouldn't I be more acceptable to the type of ladies I am trying to reach for you?"

It was no good. I knew I couldn't have peace and have my ears pierced.

I wanted to bulldoze ahead but ... the one questioning word that hung in the air between God and me was — OBEDIENCE.

I had thought obedience meant big things like going to the mission field at God's call or putting oneself to lots of inconvenience to preach the gospel.

In Aberdeen obedience was a tiny act. I cancelled my appointment with the jeweller. And one day I gave away the little gold Chinese characters that I'd bought in advance and wanted to wear so much. My disappointment ran deep.

Aberdeen with its roller-coaster autumn and Mr and Mrs Roworth's love.

Christmas with Jonathan and his laundry, my bare ears and John's love.

Chefoo in the New Year again, feeling so much better and with God's love. One morning near Easter when we had been in the mission seven whole years, I found an interesting verse in my Bible.

"Sacrifice and offering you did not desire,
     but my ears you have pierced ....."

said Psalm 40. Whatever does that mean, I wondered, and found that the Living Bible puts it "You have accepted the offer of my life-long service." The concept was an ancient one, dating right back to the time of the Exodus when a slave could say to his master in his seventh year of service, "I will not take my freedom though it is due to me this year. I love you, my master, and want to stay in your service." Then says the Bible, "His master shall take him ... and pierce his ear through with an awl. Then he will be his servant for life."

"You see," whispered God, "your ears are pierced already. I pierced them myself. And to me, this inner beauty counts far more than earthly jewels in there."

Wonderingly I fingered my bare lobes again, incredulous that this way they seemed good to God. "Colour me Beautiful" could be part of my life but "Colour me Beautiful on the Inside, too" was to be the main me. The gold of obedience was more important to the Lord than gilt in my ears.

# Forgive Me

*I had my schedule all planned out*
*For a well-filled busy day*
*Until I heard a still small Voice*
*Come question me and say:*
*"I had today all planned out, too;*
*Does it belong to Me or you?"*

*And then in shame I bowed my head*
*"Forgive me, Lord, I pray,*
*Hereafter I will consecrate*
*Each moment of the day;*
*And willingly I'll try to do*
*The things that You have asked me to."*

*Source Unknown*

# 16

## A dappled Christmas

"Happy Christmas, love! I'm just popping down to the school for a few moments ..."

I'm glad now that I bit back words which would condemn for ever office work at weekends, on holidays and even Christmas Day! John's tall frame reappeared in the doorway within just a few minutes. In his arms he was balancing a large brown cardboard grocery box. The ungainly package was wound round with Aunty Barb's scarlet sash, tied in a bow at the top.

"It's your Christmas present," he said, stretching the big parcel out towards me. And as I went to take it — the box mewed!

I think it must have been the best Christmas present John ever gave me. And for once I hadn't spoiled the surprise by guessing — even though John had been indiscreet enough to reveal several days earlier that he had found me the cutest little thing!

Out of that box walked Jason Coffeemate Miller. He was a Siamese sealpoint and only a few weeks old.

What a pet he was! I knew the Chefoo children

would love him when they discovered his furry presence at their school in the new term. Any excuse to be in a home would make them ask over and over again could they come up to see Jason. Hitching a lift on my shoulder, he loved to carry on curious conversations. From then until we left Chefoo I constantly revelled in this tangible evidence of God's creativity — his soft creamy fur, his delightful dark mask matching all his points in rich coffee brown. Even when he laid a love gift of an upside-down shrew on our bedroom rug I loved him, and even, yes even when he hid under the bookcase as I sang my Quiet Time hymn in the mornings!

Christmas time at Chefoo was special — excitingly special. December *and* November were encircled in the busy bustle. Christmas carols rang out early. Ned's life-size angels (shedding feathers from their wings into our dinners) hung from the dining room ceiling long before the twelfth month made its debut. Preparations, plays, programmes, parties and parcelling were exceedingly punctual, perhaps premature. And all this was because early in December Chefoo experienced an exodus. One hundred children were packed into taxis to start the twisty journey down the mountain on the first lap of their travel home. By the time our calendars indicated that December had really arrived, the atmosphere at the jungle school was tingly with anticipation like vibrations from hand-bells awaiting their next turn to ring.

The green bucket had become a hanging basket again! It was easy to spot the reasons. I was better (although my lack of energy forced on me frequent afternoon rests, much to my chagrin). With hindsight I could see what had happened to me. Gordon MacDonald in *Ordering Your Private World*, writing about health, says, "One fascinating study on stress has been conducted by Dr Thomas Holmes. Holmes's Stress Chart is a simple measurement device that indicates how much pressure a person is probably facing and how close he may be to dangerous physical and psychic consequences.

"After considerable research, various events common to all of us were assigned points by Holmes and his associates. Each point was called a 'life-change unit'. An accumulation of more than 200 of these units in one year, Holmes suggested, could be a warning of a potential heart attack, emotional stress, or breakdown of ability to function as a healthy person." (1)

Looking down through the microscope at 1975-76, I thought I *never* wanted to be 41 again. But that wasn't it. Too many stresses had built up. I had exceeded my quota. My physical make-up had demanded a retreat.

My father used to say when we were in trouble (in the beautiful old language of the Authorized Version of the Bible), "And it came to pass ..." It was true. The year of the trough passed. Even though we think we're never going to make it; never be happy again, most of us come out the other end. Just hanging in there, I knew now that my tunnel "came to pass". Christmas 1977 saw my traumas behind me.

And Jonathan had graduated to Monkton Combe Senior School. He loved it. (Basically, that is. His letters see-sawed from what a drag life was, to confessing he even enjoyed his exams.) He'd left Monkton Junior with the Aston Prize for English. Predictably, too, he won the Writing Competition year after year because his calligraphy was a second edition of John's, and he held *interesting* conversations during the summer holidays with me, such as this one:

J:      Mum, when your time is up in Malaysia,
        would you and Dad not consider working
        somewhere else in the Far East for OMF? Like
        the Philippines, for example?

Me:     Oh yes. When our ten-year visa runs out, we
        are completely open for what the Lord asks us
        to do.

J:      I thought you said you'd be going home soon.

Me:     No. Not necessarily. We've no leading about
        the future yet.

J:      Good!

Me:     Why?

J:      I like spending my summer holidays out here!

   More recently he would have added, "Check it
out, baby!"

   When he left at the summer's end, I was able, at
least, to give two cheers for September. John and I
actually sang on our way back from the airport. Not in
glee, of course, but because God had so ably flipped
the coin of our lives. We motored back to Chefoo with
a whole new teenage vocabulary; back to the bulletin
still stuck on the wall of our mountain home.

NOTICE
WHILE IN THIS ROOM SPEAK IN
A LOW SOOTHING TONE AND DO NOT
DISAGREE WITH ME
IN ANY MANNER!

Please be informed that when one has reached "MY
AGE", Noise and Non-Concurrence cause gastric
Hyper-peristalsis, Hyper-Secretion of Hydrochloric
Acid, and rubus of the Gastric Mucosa and I become
MOST UNPLEASANT!!

He had stretched incredibly, too — four inches nearer
the sky than I! And his voice oscillated from treble to
deep bass. "My giddy aunt," he would croak (or

squeak), when he fluffed a shot on the golf course. I had found Jonathan Neil Miller, age 14, a new experience. Mothering a teenager brought a palette full of freshly blended colour into my life.

Christmas 1977 was to be our first Christmas apart. He was going to his hostel parents, Fred and Margaret, whom we all loved, at Donnington Hurst. I wondered if his voice had totally broken. I wondered if his brown hair was still shoulder length! I wondered if he'd thrash issues out with the other young folk such as he'd introduced in a letter; "Are you sure you aren't being deceived by Christianity? How do you know that your work at Chefoo is not a form of escapism?"

And yet, although we weren't together, I wrote in my diary that it was the happiest of Christmasses. That wasn't just because of my kitten! It was the joy of the children — children like Rachel.

It took a whole weekend to see them off, our goodbye clocks regulated by the times taxis were to meet trains and aircraft heading for different destinations. By Sunday afternoon, the playing area was beginning to wear an empty air. Only the Thai party was left — thirty children who would set off at midnight down through the dark hairpin bends to catch a train near the border of Thailand at 8 a.m.

The small "waiters" played excited games in a deserted campus. Would it ever be time to be awakened from their cosy beds, to be fed a travel tablet, to shiver and dress, dress and shiver in the cold night air, to call "Happy Christmas" to teachers and dorm aunties waving under the carbon sky? How could the clock be persuaded to tick a bit faster?

A little shiny-eyed princess danced up to me as I crossed the netball court. Clutching my hand she whispered, "Mrs Miller, oh Mrs Miller, do you know what I'd like?"

"I think you'd like the taxi to arrive right now and whisk you off at a hundred miles an hour for home!" I laughed.

No. That wasn't it. And Jason Coffeemate was still hidden away as a surprise for the 25th, so it wasn't him either.

"I'd like to come up to *your* house," breathed the princess.

Inwardly I sighed a little. Ends of terms were busy — dreadfully busy. Staff members reeling with tiredness found it easiest to let the children have free play outside. Besides, would I be guilty of favouritism if I invited one little seven-year-old into our home to the envy of all her playmates?

I prevaricated and she danced away.

That familiar sense of unease when I had doubts about a course of action descended on me like the white witch. During our years at Chefoo I had made so many mistakes, selfish mistakes when I'd put what I wanted to do before the needs of others. We had chuckled delightedly at one conversation overheard in the senior girls' dorm:

"Me first," called out a blonde, racing with her comb to the top of the hair-brushing queue.

"The Bible says, 'Others first'," responded her friend, "and I'm the other."

*Okay*, I thought, *I'd laughed, but it was pretty typical of me.*

"Let's have them all up," suggested John when I told him about the little girl down on the playground. "I'll make a quick batter and we'll give them pancakes. They'll love the Christmas tree lights and we'll tell them a story. It will help to pass the time for them."

john loved the Christmas tree lights, too. He played with them incessantly, changing bulbs here and there to make them flash more brilliantly!

Soon our bungalow was packed with potential angels in playclothes, cross-legged on the rug, their eyes reflecting fairy-lights and the magic in the air. As they settled for a Dr Zeuss story on the overhead projector, I made for the rocking chair where I thought there'd be breathing space.

The little princess climbed on my knee.

Happiness is Christmas with a Chefoo child in your lap! We were all terribly glad to be alive. John's camera clicked to capture the afternoon for ever on film. What pleasure I have in that photograph now and — a certain postcard. Pleasure because I could so easily have passed up that little girl's Christmas request. I had my own ideas about what I wanted to achieve during a day, even if it was only a suntan. And I liked weekends to myself.

But by Christmas 1977 I was trying to leave misty-flat attitudes far behind me. In His mercy, God caused me to sense with the inner ear that Sunday afternoon at Chefoo. He helped me to see beyond my weekend timetable. And I am glad.

Glad because that little princess never again came dancing up to me with a request. I didn't ever see her any more. At the end of the holidays she wasn't with the Thai party when they came back to Chefoo. Rachel Gordon-Smith was killed with her whole family in a tragic road accident near Manorom Christian Hospital during the Christmas vacation. (2) A loving heavenly Father welcomed her into *His* home.

Not many days after the news of this great loss reached us, the postman brought a card for John from Thailand. A very precious card. It was from Rachel.

"Thank you," she had written in large lower-case letters, "Thank you for a lovely, lovely term at Chefoo."

Suppose I had acted Sheila-Not-Available... Suppose I had cocooned myself in my quiet corner ... Suppose I had given in to that old misty-flats nature of mine ... How should I have coped with a nightmare memory?

Instead a loving Father prompted us to host an extra end-of-term party. He painted yet another colour into my life. I think it was dappled. A Christmas with light and shade. But the memories are cloudless.

(1) Ordering Your Private World,
    Highland Books, p.32
(2) This story is told in In His Time by Eileen Gordon
    Smith, OMF Books

# The Road Not Taken

*Two roads diverged in a yellow wood,*
*And sorry I could not travel both*
*And be one traveler, long I stood*
*And looked down one as far as I could*
*To where it bent in the undergrowth;*

*Then took the other, as just as fair,*
*And having perhaps the better claim,*
*Because it was grassy and wanted wear;*
*Though as for that, the passing there*
*Had worn them really about the same,*

*And both that morning equally lay*
*In leaves no step had trodden black.*
*Oh, I kept the first for another day!*
*Yet knowing how way leads on to way,*
*I doubted if I should ever come back.*

*I shall be telling this with a sigh*
*Somewhere ages and ages hence:*
*Two roads diverged in a wood, and I —*
*I took the one less traveled by,*
*And that has made all the difference.*

*Robert Frost*

# 17
# *A Yellow Wood*

M r Walker-Brash considered the x-ray with an experienced eye. The negative was life-sized. Its half-tones contrasted with the surgeon's white coat.

"How soon can you come in?" His question was directed at John who lay flat on his examination table in the Sevenoaks Hospital. "If you don't have surgery within the next month or so, you're going to lose a kidney."

John made an effort to gather himself together.

"And," said Mr Walker-Brash, as though it had just occurred to him, "this will mean you can never go back to the tropics again."

The silence in the consulting-room lengthened. There didn't seem to be anything John could say to that.

John's track record had been good. Strong and fit. It was just that when he did take ill, he liked to do it on a grand scale with all sorts of dramatic spin-offs. It wasn't the first time this kidney had played up.

Once in Kuala Lumpur our gracious and much-loved director, Don Fleming, almost flew him to hospital with what seemed like acute appendicitis. Due to the uncivilized hour of the night and our panic in racing John towards medical care, the three of us forgot our wallets. Perhaps we were still geared to Britain's National Health Service. Anyway we had no deposit except John himself so he was relegated to a third-class ward where Westerners seldom appeared.

It wasn't appendicitis after all. He had renal cholic and eventually passed the stone. Any kidney complaint means the patient has to drink, drink, drink. So over John's bed a bulletin read "FLUIDS + + +"

"Could I have a glass of water?" asked John weakly on noticing the instructions.

The little Malay nurse shook her head. "Sorry. The cupboards with the mugs are all locked up," she explained, "otherwise the patients take them and soon we don't have any for people who ask."

The sister in the ward required John to wear hospital pyjamas. The pyjamas looked like flour bags. They were also made for Asians. Asians are petite. The pyjama legs barely stretched to John's knees. When the claustrophobic heat entreated him push back the top sheet these knees presented themselves for all onlookers. In addition to being tall and thin, John's skin is exceedingly fair. It has the appearance of translucent milk opal. As his bed was at the far end of the ward by the door, he was right on the pedestrian traffic route — sepia-coloured pedestrian traffic.

You could almost hear their minds click as they did a double-take. What was that? An "orang putih" (white man)? *VERY* "putih"! And they'd come back to inspect the milk opal legs with their fair hair — just to check that it hadn't been a vision.

John's fascination with life in this third-class ward was passed on to his visitors. All of us were intrigued.

That policeman over there, for instance — *he* was on guard by a bed. The patient was a prisoner. Did the Tamil Indians *always* shake their heads vigorously when they talked? We watched the warmhearted Malay nurses who grinned at John's basic conversations with them in their own language. I grinned at that too. John had a superb vocabulary of words like roofs, doors, floors, walls, windows, ceilings etc because he had overseen the building of our new staff house at Chefoo. But how he was coping with "thermometer", "medicine" and "bed-pan" I couldn't imagine.

The bathroom, when John did make it, was — well, awash. John would trek the long length of the ward to reach it, the cynosure of every brown eye. As he splashed through the water in his flip-flops, it was impossible not to wonder where it had come from.

Clanging a tin can of tea, a vendor dropped in from the street well before dawn each morning. Not a convenient time for owls. Sick owls. "Tea! Anyone for tea?" he yelled. "Yes," John would reply wearily, "if I'd something to put it in."

That was one of our yesterdays — in our first term of service at Chefoo.

But during our second four years, John repeated the drama. This time it was a ten-hankie-act and we started off in the Camerons. He nearly scared us all senseless by being carried out of the bedroom on a stretcher. A visual aid for his sermon, "The Man with Ten Legs". Dass, our gardener, Andrew, an old Chefusian (himself white-faced after seeing the tiger at the school gate), Tim and Linton from staff hung on to the stretcher's corners as they manoeuvred John down to the car. The hospital lay a mere one hundred and forty miles away. It was a shaky night for me when "they" thought John had TB. Then they were suspicious of that kidney again. In trying to diagnose the trouble, they managed to puncture the bladder wall performing a biopsy.

That night John was so ill that I tried to come to terms with what it would be like to lose him. I just about wore the monogram off my ten hankies.

But that was yesterday, too. John had finished his Chefoo career at a fantastic farewell party organized by the staff in total secrecy. We were treated to ridiculous skits about leprachauns, infamous Irish jokes and strange lyrics, one composed by Linton for the occasion. It lilted along to the tune of MacNamara's Band and verses from it went something like this:

> "Oh their names are John and Sheila, if it's
>     golf you want to try
> Give John a game, and to your shame,
>     you'll find your score is high,
> He's a big hit in the Camerons — and if
>     you want the proof
> They say that he can hit a birdie on the
>     temple roof!
>
>
> "Oh their names are John and Sheila, they're the
>     leaders of the band
> A band we all agree is quite the best band in the
>     land,
> Though you've been unwell for quite a spell,
>     we've prayed you out of bed
> But just in time for furlough, wouldn't you
>     rather stay instead?"

Dear gifted Linton with his blarney! Come to think of it — the tune wasn't bad either! We loved the

Chefoo staff as well as the children!

Now in 1981 Chefoo was a memory — a golden one. As our time there drew to a close John had been invited to take the Assistant Home Director's post at Belmont, The Vine, Sevenoaks. Sevenoaks was the new location for the British headquarters of OMF. The Newington Green premises in London were also a memory — sold amid a great deal of nostalgia.

Sevenoaks, a dormitory town for London, snuggled in a pretty picture-postcard setting in Kent. Charing Cross Station lay only half-an-hour away by train. "The Vine" (not OMF Belmont, Devine as one envelope was addressed) was the glorious cricket ground just opposite, where the first game of English cricket was said to have been played, overlooked by its seven sturdy oaks. Guy Longley, our Central Office Executive Secretary was teased unmercifully during the summer. Somehow he managed to write his receipts at a desk, centre front by the window!

John and I delighted in the sunny flat above the offices. Our two years in Sevenoaks teemed with rich experiences for me. My hobby had become my job. At long last I was able to attend stimulating sessions at the Fellowship of Christian Writers, London's Christians in the Arts Centre, Writing for Pleasure classes with my friend Jean who was a real professional, and dabbling in crafts like the Patchwork Course I took with Kathleen, the Home Director's wife. At Easter my feelings bled through a poignant performance of the Bach St Matthew Passion in the Royal Festival Hall. In London, we even met Cliff Richard after all my years of adulation, for to me, there's a whole wide spectrum of music to be enjoyed.

It was in this setting that John introduced Act Three. The kidney stone forming in Malaysia now presented itself as a "staghorn calculus". That was when Mr Walker-Brash entered the scene. So it meant hospitalization yet again, where John was almost sliced in half and lay looking like the colour of those faraway flour bags.

It really didn't seem likely that we'd ever be in the Far East again.

But meanwhile, John Wallis our new Home Director had a letter from Singapore. Please could he release John to work on the directorate at International Headquarters?

John W visited John M in hospital. He thought John looked as though he wasn't going anywhere ever again. So he kept quiet about the letter. Was there a large red traffic light signalling STOP?

News of that letter greeted John with the force of an atomic bomb two months later. That's what heralded his return to work in the Sevenoaks office.

Mr Walker-Brash gave advice and made helpful comments. "Well," he considered, "I think I should refer you to the University Hospital in London. Let the physician there give his opinion about Singapore."

OMF's Medical Officer at International Headquarters, Dr Monica, had seen the two of us through several crises by now. Again she felt prepared to take the risk. Singapore was a medical hub with specialists tucked into consulting suites ad infinitum. John, accompanied by her letter, boarded a train for London. And that was when the red light changed to amber.

My enthusiasm for another adventure with God threatened, at first, to overrule all commonsense. Singapore! OMF's fulcrum!

"Sheila! We're not catching the next plane!" John applied the brakes. "Let's think this through prayerfully. Let's ask the opinions of others."

Amber lights are difficult to live through. Our Sevenoaks niche had captivated me — just like *Heatherlea, Hey There* and Chefoo did. Moving out again ...? Well? Perhaps it was a bit premature to get excited. Just then, taking us totally by surprise, John received two invitations urging him to apply for principalships of schools in the South of England.

"I think I prefer school desks to office ones," John stated uncertainly.

Jonathan, too, had misgivings. He'd grown out of OMF's hostel. He was at University now. He had been glad to have Sevenoaks as his pad. Where would he live for half-terms and holidays?

And then OMF sent me for my medical check up. I found the new doctor dour. "You've a body battered by drugs," he stated. (Medication, I expect a lay person would say.) "You could do with spending the rest of your life in a country cottage, where pressures on your insulted womanhood would lessen."

I lay on his examination table, feeling like a floppy disc, left on the shelf instead of slotted into a place of usefulness. Despairingly, I watched him write up his notes. Would OMF accept a pessimistic prognosis like this? Me — a city girl, (despite my years hidden in the jungle), relegated to viewing roses from behind lace curtains? Me — still in my mid-forties? I felt as though I'd been dropped on a rubbish tip.

The journey back to Belmont from his surgery was grim. By the time we reached home, my gloom was darkening to morose melancholy. And then, like a precious pencil-shaft of God's sunlight, I recalled Psalm 34: "I will extol the Lord at all times; his praise will always be on my lips." Bringing a bouquet to my Maker bailed me out of the blues as so often before.

Yet we did feel uncertain about the way ahead. John wasn't sure that he liked administration. Wasn't a principal's desk a good option? Jonathan wanted a home *at* home. I thought I liked the Singapore idea but the doctor had advised me to try tending roses.

We felt like Robert Frost who wrote, "The Way Not Taken".

"Two roads diverged in a yellow wood,
    And sorry I could not travel both ..."

One morning John carried his Bible into the sunny kitchen to share his midnight thoughts with me.

"It's these verses in Leviticus, Sheila," he said. "I can't get away from them."

I looked over his shoulder. "... the fire must be kept burning on the altar ..." said the Lord to Moses.

"It comes up three times," explained John. "Look, 'The fire on the altar must be kept burning; *it must not go out*' and 'The fire must be kept burning on the altar *continuously*; it must not go out.' Sheila, do you notice how it's reiterated and amplified?"

I remembered how John had preached on Barnabas a few Sundays previously. I had felt we could slot *our* names into Acts 13 verse 2. Set apart for me John and Sheila for the work to which I have called them.

"John, I think it's a post with bite in it. At the desk of Director for Personnel you'd be challenged to the hilt! If God is leading, I'd really love to go."

My medical report? It never turned up. Somewhere along the line it got lost and somehow it managed to stay lost! Nobody seems to know where or how.

Again Robert Frost echoed our sentiments. Chefoo had been a way "less traveled by". We doubted if we, too, could ever turn back.

"Two roads diverged in a wood, and I —
    I took the one less traveled by,
    And that has made all the difference."

# Prayer

*Master, they say that when I seem*
*To be in speech with you,*
*Since you make no replies, it's all a dream*
*— One talker aping two.*

*They are half right, but not as they*
*Imagine; rather, I*
*Seek in myself the things I meant to say,*
*And lo! the wells are dry.*

*Then, seeing me empty, you forsake*
*The Listener's role, and through*
*My dead lips breathe and into utterance wake*
*The thoughts I never knew.*

*And thus you neither need reply*
*Nor can; thus, while we seem*
*Two talking, thou art One forever, and I*
*No dreamer, but thy dream.*

C S Lewis

# 18

# The Green Light

My favourite room in Belmont's flat was the kitchen. A long Victorian sash window above the sink overlooked the Vine cricket pitch. Strange how we all offered to wash up in the summer!

The window highlighted a solid oak table and an antique oven — both rescued from the Newington Green guest house (although I never quite understood the reasoning behind salvaging the latter).

Before most noble Britishers surfaced for the day, I'd sit at that oak table and watch the sun begin to hit my pin-ups of Cliff. By breakfast-time even the clock on the next wall would be radiant. The kitchen was a halcyon haven for "Quiet Times".

"Heavenly Father," I said to God one morning the following autumn, before the sun had made it, "if John wasn't called to Singapore, the place I'd like to go is Israel."

Of course, in actual fact, I was prepared to follow John to the ends of the earth. But I knew what put this unusual thought in my mind. My Bible reading had been in the prophets. All that was going to happen to

Israel in the last days fired my imagination. I thought I saw it all beginning before my very eyes.

I had been alive in 1938 when Hitler determined to wipe out every Jewish person he could lay his hands on. Six million of God's people were brutally murdered. *Yet*, ten years later David ben Gurion was putting Israel back in the school atlas. The death and rebirth of a nation! It was exciting. Wouldn't it be good to live where it was all happening?

After Jonathan had finished his A-levels at Monkton Combe School, he wanted to travel for a year before entering university. Conversations in our Belmont flat vacillated from whether he should try his hand at sheep-farming in Australia, to the call of the South American ranches, disembarking at several venues en route. Opportunities for students were spirit-stirring. Jonathan planned to work on a building site to earn his fare.

"Mum, if you were me, where would you go?" he asked one day.

"Israel," I replied without a doubt. "That's where the action is."

Jonathan was switched on. He ended up in a kibbutz near Tel Aviv, milking four hundred cows every day (by machinery).

At one stage he wrote to say that an American dental student on the kibbutz was going home via Britain. Could she stay with us overnight?

The letter arrived *after* Miriam.

And I didn't realize at first that I was entertaining my first Jewess. Northern Ireland wasn't like Toronto, New York, Perth or London with a large Jewish population (although I delight in tracing just the slightest of Irish accents in President Chaim Herzog's voice!). Until this point I had had very little exposure to Jewish folk. My interest in Israel descended from my mother who loved God's chosen people and had observed the rebirth of the nation after the war with joy.

Miriam came through for breakfast as I was poring over my Bible in the sunny kitchen. It seemed the most natural thing in the world to share with her what I was reading. And I prayed to Israel's great God, committing this enchanting girl to Him as she resumed her travels.

As I raised my head, I saw that her eyes were full of tears.

"You see, Lord," I said that autumn morning months later, "I would like to share your Word with lots more Jewish girls. I don't think many Jewish people know much about You nowadays. Perhaps I could teach them from their own Scriptures."

All at once an unusual thought hit me. *You don't need to go to Israel to read the Bible with Jewish women.*

The sun's rays shone on the solid oak table. They shone on me and I lit up like I usually do with one of my new ideas.

*Yes,* continued my thoughts, *remember Valerie Griffiths? She used to hold a Bible Study in her Singapore flat. It was for Japanese ladies. But she wasn't in Japan!*

My thoughts, captivated by this new notion, surged ahead. *Well, if the last General Director's wife could hold a Bible Study for Japanese ladies at International Headquarters, couldn't I have one for Jewish girls?*

It was at this point I put a foot on the brakes. I had always been so grateful to my father for passing his sound common sense on to me. Where had it gone?

*Inside a few moments,* I chided myself, *you have dreamed up a Bible group in a flat you haven't reached, with people you don't know exist in Singapore. You don't even know if there's a synagogue there. Look at it logically, Sheila. Would Israelis settle between Malaysia and Indonesia — both predominantly Muslim countries? No. Most unlikely!*

*And even if they did, how would you find them? Singapore's population is 2.5 million. Do you propose to ring the Israeli Embassy (if there is one) for a list of names and addresses? Don't be ridiculous!* And I tried to dismiss the idea.

But that idea refused to go away. *Perhaps,* I thought, time after time, day after day, *there are Jewish people in Singapore.*

"John," I started one morning, holding tightly on to my courage. "I've had a way-out idea ..."

"What have you thought up now, Sheila?"

"It's just that *this* one won't go away. I'm beginning to wonder if perhaps ..."

"Perhaps what?"

"Do you think it's not one of my crazy ideas? Do you think it may be the inner voice of the Holy Spirit?"

That morning we decided that I should get in touch with "The Church's Ministry Among the Jews" and "Prayer for Israel", two societies I felt could send me some books and cassettes — just *in case* the thoughts had come from God.

Back came quite a load of literature and a superb tape by David Pawson called, "The time has come for the Gentiles to repay their debt to the Jews." I felt more inspired than ever.

Into our trunks, lining the Belmont landing, went all this info, including a manual on how to get to know your Jewish friends. I had no Jewish friends.

Having attended to the demands of the idea, I became absorbed in packing and celebrating Christmas. Jonathan came down from the University of Durham where he was majoring in Geography. Despite the great gaps in his knowledge that early Monkton report had indicated, it was his favourite subject! For John and me December 1981 held days when the amber light was changing to green. Feverishly, as usual, we were tackling another sort-out of our bits and pieces — getting ready to GO.

And January 1982 saw me focusing once more on the familiar banana fronds as our jet headed for the new runways of Changi Airport, Singapore.

I hadn't even surfaced from jet-lag when Judy, the guest home hostess, began to chat to me. It was in the OMF Suzuki, our little car, like a motorbike with a roof on it. We were en route to our welcome picnic down near the waterfront.

Some people experience visions. Some folk see "pictures". Others speak a word of prophecy or say they "heard" a voice. I just have ideas. Goose-pimples bumped up on my sticky arms when Judy said, a propos of nothing, "Sheila, I know another Sheila in Singapore. I think you two should get together. She has a terrific interest in Israel and has lots of Jewish friends."

The Suzuki with our husbands in front found its way to the picnic spot. Judy chatted on beside me with her smallest daughter wriggling on her knee, but I remember nothing except the mind-boggling words about her other friend Sheila. She had no idea she had blown out all my lights. However, as soon as possible, I asked her to come down for coffee so that I could disclose to her my delightful secret.

"We must get together at once," Judy exclaimed and within a few days Sheila M met Sheila P.

We talked — exciting, challenging exchanges.

"I must tell you this," said Sheila P. "You won't have known it. My husband is being drafted home to England. I have been praying that God would send somebody else to take an interest in my Jewish contacts!"

Think of it! Eight thousand miles away, God was working on answering this beautiful girl's prayer. By February she was introducing me to her friends.

Sheila plunged me in at the deep end. "Do you know what!" she exclaimed. Her enthusiasm was catching. "We'll have a Farewell Party for me. I'll invite the guests and *you* can be the hostess!"

That just about threw me for a loop. Entertaining is not my thing! The list of Jewish visitors threatened *panic*. The crisis was nicely enveloped in excitement and joy, though. Anne, my neighbour upstairs, rescued me. Among other talents, Anne has the gift of "helps". She could even cope with Kosher food and lent me her elegant china Royal Doulton dinner service.

"Now," I explained, "as I began to serve the buffet lunch, "I want you all to know that there's no animal fat in any of this food; no pork ..."

"Pity!" said one after another and — the ice was broken.

That day we sent Sheila P off with the words from Psalm 121 ringing in all our ears:

"The Lord watches over you ...
   The Lord will watch over your coming and going
      both now and forever more."

and I had the great joy of praying my first prayer with them. It was the priestly blessing from the Torah, in Numbers 6:

"The Lord bless you and keep you;
   The Lord make his face shine upon you

and be gracious to you;
the Lord turn his face toward you
and give you peace."

I knew I was meant to be launched but it was to be months yet before bridges of friendship were built strongly enough to suggest Bible studies.

The bridges-of-friendship bit was tremendous. That's when I met Barbara, Grace and Morag — Christians who also loved Israelis. Grace and Morag had been two of Sheila P's guests at our farewell luncheon. Grace introduced me to Barbara.

Barbara was an elegant American who lived in an absolute mansion. She reminded me of the centurion who said to the Lord Jesus, "I myself am a man ... with soldiers under me. I tell this one, 'Go,' and he goes; and that one, 'Come,' and he comes. I say to my servant 'Do this,' and he does it." Anyway Barbara knew two of the Jewish ladies well enough to ask them to teach us Hebrew songs from the Scriptures.

I don't think I'll ever forget those mornings. "I sat up nearly all night," said Hannah, the singer, "looking through my Bible to find out where these words are from. I was sure you'd ask me!" And this Jewish girl taught us beautiful tunes to words like these:

Hineh ma tov
Umah na'im
Shevet achim
gam yachad

from Psalm 133, "How good and pleasant it is when brothers live together in unity!"

*It's true*, I reflected. Sarah kept popping up and down to take photographs at one of our lunches saying, "It's not so long ago that Christians were persecuting Jews. Now here we are praying for Israel together!"

"Hannah," I asked over coffee, one morning after our singalong, "Is there any Israeli tune to words from the prophet Isaiah?

"Like what?"

"I was thinking of Isaiah chapter 53."

Hannah opened her Bible and read the whole chapter aloud in Hebrew.

As she snapped the precious book shut, she didn't answer my question. She just thoughtfully said, "It does sound like Jesus, doesn't it?"

Barbara, Grace, Morag and I decided we should pray together on the Thursday mornings we weren't singing. We felt we were hanging on to the tail of a rocket that was just about to take off.

I loved the mornings we went to Barbara's house. It was so good to kneel on her Persian carpet. Carpets were pluralised all over her beautiful home. I had never seen anything quite like it. The only simile I could suggest was some glorious set on TV for the million dollar movie of the year. At the foot of her circular staircase a fountain cascaded, as the back-up to our music. Outside the airconditioning, her swimming pool glinted in the Singapore sun.

Then it was my turn to have the prayer meeting in Flat A, 2 Cluny Road. Barbara, Grace and Morag were all charismatically inclined. It was never good enough to sit on the settee to pray. One by one we'd slip to the floor with bowed heads.

Our simple flat had a bare brown-tiled floor. One day, a missionary going on study-leave called.

"Sheila, I wondered if you'd like to babysit our rug while we're away," she offered.

I was delighted. I expressed my appreciation in glowing terms. It matched the floor exactly.

"You must come down and see it in situ," I said.

Linnet looked at her own rug on our floor. Then she looked at me. "As you really like it," she confided, "I think I'll risk telling you its history."

Aghast, I heard Linnet explain that her husband had delivered the rug from the fate of being turfed on to a rubbish tip, by rescuing it from a pile of trash in a neighbour's garden. He had shampooed it and set it up like new (almost).

Well, when I saw Barbara's elegant forehead touching our rescued-from-the-rubbish-bin, mud-coloured mat, I just about came unglued.

But those mornings were precious and the following February we were ready to wade deeper. We celebrated the Feast of Purim with seven Jewish girls and four of us (at Barbara's). They were going to tell us about their customs on that day and I was going to take my first Bible study with them on Esther.

What is a Jewish Bible study?

I only know what it is not. It isn't everyone sitting around formally, as Christians often do, quietly listening.

And yet I was really prepared to talk to them. *Over* prepared! I had so much to share about how the prophet Isaiah describes our good deeds as filthy rags but — God has provided garments of salvation for us: just as one day Queen Esther came before King Ahasuerus, dressed in the royal robes *he* had given *her*, to beg for mercy. She had reached out and touched his sceptre of acceptance.

At lunch I had whispered to Sarah, "Are you able to stay for the story of Esther?"

"Wouldn't miss it!" she replied.

So I launched in to my attention-grabbing intro-duction. Just when I felt confident that I had won their interest, Sarah rose from her antique chair, crossed the carpet through the cigarette smoke in front of me and made a telephone call from the other side of the room. I struggled on while Hava beside me kept a careful eye over my shoulder on my notes, like an inquisitive robin.

But it was a beginning.

In those early days Barbara and I formed a delightful partnership using any special occasion as a reason for a Bible study. Dinah was going back to Israel. So did Naomi once — with Ruth the Moabitess.

"I love this story," I told them, "because Ruth was a goya, a gentile, like me. The Apostle Paul, a Jewish intellectual, had explained that Gentiles were excluded 'from citizenship in Israel.' He said we were 'foreigners to the covenants of promise, without hope and without God in the world.'

"So you see," I concluded, "I can identify with Ruth. I was born with no right to Israel's God. Ruth needed a *goel*. So do I. So do we all. We all need a Redeemer ... " How beautiful is the gospel in the Old Testament.

It was another step forward when regular Bible studies started, just attended by a few. We drew graphs as we sat around Barbara's rosewood table, plotting the ups and downs in the lives of Bible heroes like King David or Abraham.

These structured times were peppered with wider-range coffee specials when perhaps twenty or more of us, Jews *and* Gentiles would have a get-together. One day in May we grouped in a semicircle to view a video on the Feast of Tabernacles in Jerusalem. It was an exciting thing to us that Christians had started to celebrate this feast with the Jews.

As the TV was switched off, a silence descended on our little group. It was one of those quiet moments when the Lord's presence was almost tangible.

Hannah was the one to speak first. "If our Messiah turns out to be your Jesus," she said in front of us all, "I won't be surprised." She paused. "And," she added softly, "I won't be disappointed." The thought of Jewish believers is precious. Gentile Christians are a different race of people. But a Jewish believer will always be a Jew — only more so than ever.

That year John and I went for a short leave in June. We were away for four months. On our return, I discovered that Hannah had left Singapore. She had gone back to Israel. I've never seen her again.

One day, too, dear Barbara announced that she and her family were going home — returning to America. Singapore's expatriate population constantly changes. One by one, also, most of those first contacts slipped out of my life — back to Israel — with Bibles. Mid-year was the worst. I was left wondering how to start again every October.

Somehow the Lord has always stepped in, bringing me fresh opportunities, new Jewish friends and the help of Darlene, a young American housewife who deeply loves the God of Israel.

A Jewish Bible study in Singapore? Often in our flat? Singapore is an island where dreams come true — dreams inspired by Israel's great God.

# Rose-coloured Christmas

*Holly wintered wine-bottle green*
*swaddling red.*
*Sage green with breadcrumbs.*
*And pearly spotted mistletoe.*

*Woody log-brown*
*wearing a white waxy candle.*
*Basted turkey-bronze.*
*Postman parcel-brown*
*with this year's rainbow-hued stamps.*

*Golden candle glow*
*dispelling deep-dyed December violet.*
*And pied fairy lights*
*decking frost-spangled cones.*

*A spectrum of colours*
*diffracted from a prismatic manger*
*where The Light lay*
*gloom-girdled, bleak-byred.*

Sheila Miller

# 19

# Rose-coloured Spectacles

It was December. The grey light of dawn was barely chasing the shadows in the sitting room. Although the morning was grey, it wasn't chill because Singapore is almost on the equator. The chill I felt was inward — my mind was full of a family problem.

I switched on the fan and turned my attention to my Quiet Time books. The Bible passage before me was the story of the loaves and fishes from John Chapter 6. A well-worn account. How could this miracle touch me today in my dilemma?

Jonathan, still studying at university in England, was wondering where he could spend Christmas. OMF had cared for him beautifully in providing a hostel for holidays and sometimes paid his fare to visit us — until he was eighteen. But now he was "grown-up", or almost, and had nowhere to go.

Perhaps this last statement isn't quite accurate. No relatives were around but one or two kind people had suggested he spend Christmas with them. He sent us an airform, asking what he should do, and our hearts ached with longing for him ourselves. Perhaps this was the very last year he'd be "young" enough to belong to *us* for Christmas. And we'd seen so little of him in the last nine years. Perhaps ... But ... The "but" was the expense involved. We didn't have the fare.

I turned back to the loaves and fishes. "Jesus ... said to Philip, 'Where shall we buy bread for these people to eat?' He asked this only to test him, for already He had in mind what He was going to do. Philip answered Him. 'Eight months' wages would not be enough ...' Andrew spoke up, 'Here is a boy with five small barley loaves and two small fish, but how far will they go among so many?'"

I knew the words so well. I could almost have set the Bible aside and recited them. In the commentary I was using Dr Campbell Morgan wrote, "Philip did not answer the question as to the 'where'". "He said in effect, 'What is the use of talking about 'where' when we have no money to buy?'" In the grey December morning, his query echoed my own thoughts. It was as if I had read, "What is the point of discussing all the 'wheres' of your son's Christmas, wishing the 'where' could be with you, if you have no money to buy the fare?"

Then Dr Morgan continued, "He asked the question to prove Philip. *He did it to give Philip his chance.* Philip's answer was the answer of calculation, with no sense whatever of the significance of the question from the standpoint of the ability of the Lord."

And right out of that grey December sky I knew the Lord was saying to me that morning, just as He had then, "Even if there is no money, I can perform a miracle."

Sitting there in the shadows, the compound still very quiet in the early morning, I sensed God's love sweep over me. The compassion of a heavenly Father, who saw our need to be together for Christmas, moved me to tears. It was as if John 6:9 read, "There is a lad here with 25 pounds," (we knew this as we had scraped the bottom of the barrel to send it), "but how far can that go when the airfare is 500 pounds?" Although it was already December and so near Christmas, the faith was born in me to ask for a multiplication miracle too. It was another of those mornings when a new idea overwhelmed me.

My feet barely touched the ground that day. I thought I'd never been happier in my life. God's love for us was so great — Jonathan was coming for Christmas ...

"Dear Father," I asked, "am I imagining this sense of Your Presence? Have You really indicated to me that we will be together for Christmas?" I'd hardly finished my prayer when a beautiful verse came to mind from the clouds where I was floating — "Blessed is she who has believed for there will be a performance of those things told her of the Lord." The verse was extra precious because it was 'feminine' and I was thrilled when I noted later that her promise was — a Son for Christmas!

Still, my faith was just that bit shaky. The days were beginning to slip past and no word of an impending flight to meet reached us. Again I asked the Lord to reassure me.

Mail is very special at Christmas time to a missionary, and I was having so much pleasure those days opening cards and letters. This one made me pause to think it all through again. Mrs Roworth, Jonathan's godmother, had written, "I've got an address from your mother for him but if my card misses him because he has joined you, I'll be *quite* happy!" What made her say that? Why would she think he'd be with us? She knew he wasn't usually. Was there a special family secret plan afoot?

Yes! That was it. It was to be a surprise! One day soon he'd just come bouncing through the door but ... I would have known all the time!

That week our interested-in-Israel group met. It was our Thursday morning prayer-meeting at Barbara's. No one knew how preoccupied my thoughts were.

Just before it was time to leave, Morag spoke. Out of the blue, I heard her say, "Sheila, I feel God wants you to know something."

I paused.

"You are to be the recipient of His gifts," she said. "He is your King."

I came home and — made up Jonathan's bed! My heart sang as I tucked his blue striped sheets around the mattress. I continued to live with shining eyes.

To me the atmosphere on our campus was high with anticipation. *All* the mothers were waiting for their children's homecoming! "Is Jonathan coming for Christmas?" Jim, alias Dr James Hudson Taylor III, our General Director, called to John in passing.

"I — I — th — think so," stammered John. He thought it would be lack of faith to say, "No, not that we know of." But ...

But time was telescoping rapidly. On the evening of December 23 John mingled with Singapore's late-night shoppers in the bright lights to tidy-up the ends of his Christmas list. I stayed at home to bake mince pies and shortbread and — besides, I wanted to be there when the taxi would arrive from the airport and my big burly, curly-headed exuberant son would come bouncing through the front door, calling "Merry Christmas, Mum and Dad!"

The telephone rang. It was a long-distance call

from OMF in Sevenoaks. "Oh, by the way," said Denis, the director on the other end of the line, "I've just been chatting here to Jonathan. He's fine."

"Wh-where is he spending Christmas?" I whispered. Denis's voice boomed over the eight thousand miles. "Why right here, I think, at the OMF centre."

With trembling fingers I replaced the receiver. The hot steamy kitchen suddenly no longer was a temple of happiness. I switched off my joyful Christmas music. And I shed tears into my pastry.

I had been so sure. There had been those other times that the Lord had spoken clearly to me like this and what He'd said had strangely happened.

This time had I claimed a promise that was not for me? Was it an idea *not* from God? I don't know. I just know that our boy didn't come. The little blue bedroom was empty and one day, shortly after Christmas, I took the striped sheets off his bed.

Jehovah Jireh had not provided.

I felt like the disciples must have done the day of the loaves and fishes miracle. Mark records that life was so hectic the Lord Jesus had promised them a holiday. "'Come with me,' He said, 'by yourselves to a quiet place and get some rest.'

"So they went away by themselves in a boat to a solitary place ..." A false hope. The crowd was keeping tabs on them. No country picnic on their own after all. Jesus had compassion for crowds. His compassion lasted the whole holiday long.

Did the disciples feel let down? There's no record of that. And as I look back on my disappointment, too, I want to record that not once did I feel jilted either.

That incident was my great opportunity to prove to God that I love Him, love Him with all my heart, even if He were never to send Jonathan out to us again. I feel that if I had had the desire of my heart at that time it would have been only natural for me to love God in the light of such a joy. But He has given me joy anyway.

I want to record with Habakkuk, "Though the fig-tree shall *not* blossom ... though there be no herd (boy) in the stall (bedroom), *yet* will I rejoice in the Lord ..." I want to say with Daniel's friends, "If we are thrown into the blazing furnace, the God we serve is able to save us from it, and He will rescue us from your hand O King! *But even if He does not*, we want you to know, O King, that we will not serve your gods or worship the image of gold you have set up."

But even if He does not ... I will worship and adore Him.

Secondly and strangely, that Christmas was the happiest I have ever known. The message of the incarnation was more precious than in any year before. I found a "new" oldie among the carols, *Cradled in a manger, meanly*. I loved these lines:

"Blessed Saviour, Christ most holy,
In a manger Thou didst rest;
Canst Thou stoop again, yet lower,
And abide within my breast?"

*Was it really worse*, I wondered, *for the Lord to make His home in me than to be born in a cave?*

Enter, then, O Christ most holy;
Make a Christmas in my heart;
Make a heaven of my manger:
It is heaven where Thou art.

And to those who never listened
To the message of Thy birth,
Who have winter, but no Christmas
Bring to them Thy peace on earth!

Supposing it was winter without Christmas like C S Lewis described in the Narnia tales ... But even on the equator we had Christmas. As I listened to Jimmy and Carol Owen's *Christmas Cantata*, the music shone like a rainbow through my tears.

*The* Light cradled in a bleak byre was diffracted into my life despite the grey of December.

Three years passed. December 1985 arrived and Jonathan was a student-on-holiday for the last time. He had just finished postgraduate studies in Journalism.

This time it was John who felt God meant us to be together for Christmas. Again, there just seemed to be no hope of that.

One day, early in the month, a message came to John's office desk. "If Mr and Mrs Miller would like to have Jonathan out for Christmas, the fare is available"!

The very last time it could ever happen to us! The *only* time it ever did.

Who that generous donor was, we don't know. All we know is that the loving kindness which prompted the gift, filled our Christmas with joy. I sat on Cloud Nine for three whole weeks! The Light cradled in a bleak byre was diffracted into our lives no matter how grey Decembers can be.

# Quiet Time

*Lord,*
*it suddenly seems crowded here*
*in the shallows where I've always*
*joyfully splashed in the*
*waters of salvation,*
*cooling myself with Your promises*
*when life gets too hot,*
*drinking the waters of grace*
*from Your hand —*
*quenching my thirst.*

*My thirst is greater now*
*and yearning toward the deep.*
*I never wanted to go in*
*over my head!*
*People drown out there —*
*die to self —*
*totally immersed in You.*

*Why did You make me*
*dissatisfied, Lord?*
*Maybe because I prayed to*
*really know You?*
*Oh, help me to move*
*toward You*

*Susan Lenzkes*

# 20

# *Epilogue*

Thirty years have passed since I read By Searching; since John Oxenham's poem of drifting on misty flats challenged me. It's seventeen years since we opted out of being "yuppies" in Ireland. I've hit my half-century! Grey strands are beginning to mingle with my black hair! I'm cultivating a silver streak. I keep reminding John that a good number of the feminine sex pay to have this put in at a hairdressing salon.

If God plotted a graph of my climb from the misty flats, it would slope upward with rather too gradual a gradient. My "high way" is a saw-toothed profile — climb for a while, stumble, rise again and then relax too long on a mini plateau. Amy Carmichael calls this the

"... subtle love of softening things
... easy choices, weakenings." (1)

but the Lord Jesus beckons me still from up and beyond, saying, "If anyone would come after me, he must deny himself and take up his cross daily and follow me." Daily.

St Paul teaches that it is we ourselves who crucify the flesh. John Stott explains, "We must not only take up our cross and walk with it, but actually see that the execution takes place." However, "having nailed our old nature to the cross, we keep wistfully returning to the scene of the execution. We begin to ... long for its release, even to try to take it down again from the cross. We need to learn to leave it there ... we are never going to draw the nails." (2)

Tucked away in the book of Jude, I've found a challenging suggestion: "Keep yourselves in God's love ..." *This is a command,* I thought. *But how do I do it? It sounds a good idea but what exactly does it mean?* Again my Living Bible proved to be a wonderful commentary on my New International Version: "Stay always within the boundaries when God's love can reach and bless you."

Life *was* like a cassette-recorder! The rewind button came into play. Again I spun back with the tape and saw myself sitting in *Hey-There's* leather armchair with The Song of Songs. Solomon had put these words into the bride's mouth, "Tell me, O one I love, where are you leading your flock today? Where will you be at noon? For I will come and join you there instead of wandering ..." That day I had planned on indulging in my favourite hobby — shopping. But what if the Heavenly Bridegroom was looking out for me at noon? I set my mind and stayed at home — because I wanted to be "within the boundaries" where His love could find me. Even shopping, like my wool for crochet, could be a distraction.

Isobel Kuhn had said, "God has no favourites." I remembered wondering, all those years ago, if this could possibly be true. How could *I* ever climb the way she did? I can't. How could *I* ever be like Amy

Carmichael? I can't. I just have to find God's special trail for me.

My upward path is etched on my mind as both an encouragement and a warning — rather like a rainbow, for a rainbow is a promise traced after a storm.

I love the God who gives me rainbows.

(1) "Make Me Thy Fuel" page 94, from Toward Jerusalem by Amy Carmichael
(2) From Only One Way by John R W Stortt (IVP)

# God the Artist

*You take the pen*
*and the lines dance.*
*You take the flute,*
*and the notes shimmer.*
*You take the brush,*
*and the colours sing.*
*So all things have mean-*
*ing and beauty*
*in that space beyond time*
*where you are.*
*How, then, can I hold*
*back anything from you?*

*Dag   Hammarskjöld*

# Acknowledgements

*Chapter 1*    Verse of "O love, that wilt not let me go" by George Matheson 1842-1906

*Chapter 2*    Died 19?, Christopher Idle, Christian Poetry, 1985

*Chapter 3*    Rainbows, © Karen Rene from Woman's Weekly 1986, reproduced with permission of the author

*Chapter 4*    Somebody Nobody, Dave Kitchen, Christian Poetry, 1978

*Chapter 5*    Out of the Mouths of Babes, Stella M Entwistle, Christian Poetry, 1978

*Chapter 6*    Chefoo, Sheila Miller, Chefoo Alumni Magazine, 1974

*Chapter 7*    A Highland Testimony, Alistair Halden, Christian Poetry, 1981

*Chapter 8*    Offering, Sheila Miller, Christian Poetry, 1977

*Chapter 9*    Reflections, Sheila Miller, Christian Herald, 1982

*Chapter 10*    Dial-a-prayer, © Luci Shaw, Listen to the Green, p.57 reproduced with permission Harold Shaw Publishers

*Chapter 11*    In No Strange Land, Francis Thomson, Collins Albatross Book of Christian Verse, p.498

Chapter 12    Donegal, © Evangeline Paterson, The Sky
              is Deep Enough, p.31 reproduced with
              author's permission

Chapter 13    Christmas is Really for the Children,
              © Steve Turner from Nice and Nasty
              reproduced with permission of Marshall
              Pickering

Chapter 14    Parting from my Son, © Evangeline
              Paterson, from Bringing the Water
              Hyacinth to Africa, Taxus Press 1983,
              reproduced by permission of the author

Chapter 15    No Scar, from Towards Jerusalem,
              Amy Carmichael reproduced by kind
              permission of SPCK, courtesy of the
              Dohnavur Fellowship

Chapter 16    Forgive Me, Source unknown
              (1) Ordering Your Private World,
                  Highland Books, p.32
              (2) This story is told in In His Time by
                  Eileen Gordon Smith, OMF Books

Chapter 17    The Road Not Taken, Robert Frost,
              Selected Poems, Penguin Books

Chapter 18    Prayer, C S Lewis Poems, Geoffrey Bles
              Ltd p.122 reproduced by permission of
              William Collins Son & Co Ltd

Chapter 19    Rose-coloured Christmas, Sheila Miller,
              Third Way, 1980

Chapter 20    Quiet Time, Susan Lenzkes, from A Silver
              Pen for Cloudy Days, Zondervan

              You Take The Pen, Dag Hammerskjold,
              Markings, translated by W H Auden and
              Leif Sjoberg, reproduced by permission
              of Faber & Faber Ltd